Anonymous

**Angling Reminiscences**

Anonymous

**Angling Reminiscences**

ISBN/EAN: 9783743347304

Manufactured in Europe, USA, Canada, Australia, Japa

Cover: Foto ©Andreas Hilbeck / pixelio.de

Manufactured and distributed by brebook publishing software (www.brebook.com)

Anonymous

**Angling Reminiscences**

# PREFACE.

THESE Sketches aspire to little more than a delineation of such occurrences as are naturally met with by lovers of the gentle craft. They are endued by the author with a colloquial form and texture, chiefly because he is of opinion that, so habited, they accord better with the spirit of the subject to which they refer. Had it been otherwise, he should not have obtruded upon a mode of composition already preoccupied by the patriarch Walton, Sir Humphrey Davy, and others. Further apology, however, he deems unnecessary, as he is not aware, throughout the following chapters, of having laid himself open to any censure as a plagiarist.

The *dramatis personæ* of his dialogue are, it may be stated, generally fictitious, although, as in most works of a similar nature, not altogether without their originals. It merits, however, no enquiry who these are, and the author disclaims all intention of throwing any light upon the subject.

To lovers of stream-side scenery, it has been attempted to render this volume acceptable, without the introduction of local details and methodical surveys. The design of the writer to embody certain ANGLING REMINISCENCES would be very inefficiently accomplished, were he to occupy the area of this small work with matters such as these. Accordingly, he has refrained from doing so as much as possible, without, it is to be hoped, impairing any of the interest which a friendly reader might otherwise have discovered in the following chapters.

---

## PUBLISHERS' NOTE TO THE PRESENT EDITION.

[This work, published in 1837, and since then become extremely scarce, is not to be confounded with either of the other two angling works by the same author. The present one is an entirely separate and distinct work. One of the other productions was published before this, and the other after it.]

# CONTENTS.

# Angling Reminiscences.

## CHAPTER I.

### INTRODUCTORY.

OUR venerable fraternity is at length dissolved! 'Tis strange, yet true. What fault had nature to find with us, save that we had lived our time? There was no unhealthiness or defection in our members— no pinings or frailties. We were, in heart, purpose, and intent, compact as ever. Alas! how freakish is fortune, leading us into treasons after happiness, and upsetting them with her finger-touch! The Angling Club at C——h is dissolved! All its kind-humoured contentions and merry assemblings, the schemes concerted for its longevity, ay, and the friendships it was wont to form, are out of being! One might naturally expect a reason for this breaking-up of interests. If

2

there were any, we never could discover it.  It lay
too deep in philosophy for our line and plummet.

>———————"'Tis wiser oft
>To leave the sources of our ills unprobed."

The Angling Club at C——h ! we are entitled to
talk of it.  It was formed originally under the auspices
of our own great-grandfather.  The armchair, in which
sat our president, was once his.  After the old man's
death, it was conveyed to our hall, and stood on a sort
of low throne at one end of the apartment, surrounded
with various implements belonging to our craft—rods,
panniers, fishing-spears, &c.

Pardon, reader, a long digression.  We have a
natural wish to say something of the ponderous arm-
chair and its revered possessor.  How rich in associations was that worm-eaten piece of furniture !  Its
quaint devices, carved in sable wood, proclaimed it
the masterpiece of some mouldered artizan, three
centuries ago; the cushion of crimson velvet, worn
and faded; its lofty Gothic architecture, with gilded
figures, Cupids and cherubim—all connected its history
with the days of old.

Alas !  the solemn heir-loom is no more !  It fell
by degrees from the hands of our club into those of a
private individual, and at length settled itself for three
long years in the back warehouse of a common pawn-
broker.  There we detected, but did not purchase it.
No !  it was already profaned by the desecrating gaze
of the many—the auctioneer had placed his unhallowed

hands upon the once-honoured relic. The heir-loom
of our club is indeed no more. We made enquiries
after its fate, and found that the crazy fabric had given
way under the sirloin of a bloated magistrate. Fire,
the devourer, has in all probability consumed the craft
of its ponderous framework—the massive limbs, with
their relief of gorgeous imagery.

But the old, thin-haired man, its occupant, have we
forgotten him ? Not so. Well we recollect the spare
bending figure of our Saturn—the visage with its
lustreless eyeballs, wrinkled cheek, and thin, sharp
nose. Well we recollect the lofty, solemn forehead,
which Time had reverenced. It was a feature of much
dignity in our aged ancestor, and contrasted strongly
with the other sunken and altered pertinents of his countenance. The freshness of youth, which had deserted
*them*, remained with *it*. Care, whose witchcraft tells
sadly upon the brows of some men, laurelled though
these be, across *his* had laid not a finger. That forehead ! We speculate upon it even to this day. It
was a portion of the genius of the past. Under its
shell had been organized the fabrics of a master
intellect ; fancy and reason had laboured at the forge
below its cavern. But it was of the past ! The
argument was over—the effect had perished with its
cause. It was of the past ! The subtle thought—the
splendid conception—the wit, eloquence, and poetry,
were each of the past !

Our great-grandfather had been what is termed a

remarkable man, but by an omission on the part of
his contemporaries, and perhaps through his own indifference, the comments upon his history are exceedingly rare. He must, however, we feel inwardly
satisfied, besides a worthy angler, have been a great
man, although neither wealth nor titles formed part of
his acquirements. The inference is drawn by us, we
know not from what quarter; it may be, indeed, that
the old arm-chair had some hand in eliciting it. This,
notwithstanding, is certain, that great as our ancestor
had been, he had met with very uncharitable treatment
from the world; for, although reputedly a voluminous
author, we had never the good fortune to stumble upon
more than a single tract, *De Fluminibus Scoticis*,
avowedly of his composition, and only once found we
mention of his name in a very old newspaper, as the
inventor of a wonderful salmon fly. The insignificance
of these discoveries nettled us not a little, but we con-
soled ourselves by the recollection, that the worthiest
frequently pass without reward, and that the humours
of critics are ofttimes lamentably touchy and capricious.
Our great-grandfather was still in our eyes a prodigy,
obscured by a cloud in its zenith, but revealed on its
horizon, ere it set, to a few privileged consecrated
gazers.

Thy second infancy, old man! was to us a solemn
lesson from Nature's volume—an instructive me-
mento reared up in our presence, to check the exu-
berance of our early follies, and bedim the dazzling

visions of our boyish enthusiasm. Tenant of the
ancient chair! thou art before us, fixed thereto like
a carved allegory;—thy shrunken limbs swathed in
rinds of flannel to ward off the chilling frosts, with
which, from the hand of Time, old age is assailed!
Vain precaution! strengthless defence! thou shiver-
est even at thy fireside; the tale of thy heart is almost at a close; its passions are over; the pulse
throbs slowly away. Thy mind wanders, old man!
Conning over the archives of its eventful history,
thou talkest like a dreamer. What connection have
these disjointed thoughts with the business of to-
day? They loiter far behind it, and are dark as
prophecy. Yet, in reverence to the tones of the
dying oracle, we listen, our own interpreter. Dote
not they to thy children's children, entering into
their hearts like counsel from a gravestone?

Our ancestor was beyond, in age, his garrulous
and whimsy days — his prate, the prate of four-
score, had ceased. He was a century old, and the
very wishes of humanity were cancelled from his
heart. All the obstinacy of a polemic temperament
lay subdued within him — he had become like a
willow in the hand of nature. Had we placed him
in his coffin, he would scarcely have discovered it;
but as yet, he looked more to advantage in the
old massive arm-chair; it suited him like a part of
his own wardrobe. The long, blue, silk dressing-
gown, contrasted well with its crimson velvet,

and the small pendant cap which confined his scanty locks was self and same with the latter material.

Our great-grandfather did not live on air. He required to be fed, and sometimes we marvelled at the appetite of the old man; he ate like a boy in his teens, and swallowed his wine-gruel with wonderful avidity. But it was a mechanical appetite after all—the palate was gone, and the functions of the stomach at a stand. Had you offered him gravel, he would have gaped for it, and exerted his gums upon pease-straw. The exercise of eating, however, sustained him; his jaw-bones kept him alive.

Very old men necessarily lose many of their faculties, and our ancestor was in a manner both deaf and blind. He heard and saw, however, by fits; and frequently would nod to an angling acquaintance, and such only, in an automaton fashion, without offering a single sign of further recognition. To some, it seemed strange how suddenly he could relapse into a state of the most absolute indifference, erecting himself slightly in his chair, and fixing his rigid eyeballs upon the opposite side of the apartment. Now, that we recollect, he breathed his last in this very position. We were sitting along with him, engaged in the perusal of an amusing book, and ever and anon casting our eyes towards the venerable chair which he occupied, little suspecting how silently within its confines death was at work, when a slight deviation from the perpendicular attitude, usual to the aged man, happened to attract our attention, and we rose up with a view to arrange the various cushions by which he was commonly supported during his last infirmity. Alas! our ancestor was already no more! The patriarchal spirit had departed out of him;—we were busying ourselves with a stiff, uncomplying corse.

Is there any virtue in the blenched lock of an old man's hair? We preserved it sacred in our bureau; it is mingled with a young girl's tresses, the offering of one who is also at rest for ever! No, not for ever! The grave will unentomb its saints, and the infant lead forth the ancient. Our great-grandfather slept for some years in the family vault below St. L——'s church; his ashes were at length disturbed by certain repairs of the building taking place. We have never discovered to what spot they happened to be removed, being abroad at the time of their resurrection; and who, alas! exists, ourselves excepted, to attach any interest to those violated remains?

But enough: Our ancestor was the founder of our club, aye, and a good angler to boot, of the old horse-hair school. We have some of his flies in our possession. They are so mis-shapen by moths that we can form no opinion of their pristine virtues. The wires are ponderous and clumsy, but in the main exquisitely tempered.

Of the exact year when the original fraternity at C——h was first instituted, there is no authentic record; neither have we discovered any documents leading us to suppose, that a narration of its proceedings was entrusted to the management of a secretary, until very lately before its dissolution. Our grandfather, who, along with our older ancestor, was a keen and competent angler, introduced us into the club, when only ten years of age; the chief requisition being, that the entrant should have slain a salmon on Tweedside. This feat we actually did accomplish at that early period of our boyhood, although (we make the confession without a blush) after the fish had been fixed and exhausted by the tackle of our grandsire, who good-naturedly conceded to us the triumph of hauling it ashore.

The club, at the time of our admission, consisted of a circle of greybeards, several of them octogenarians, and none under sixty years of age. Its numbers, as far as we recollect, were about seven or eight, all jovial fellows, full of humour, and of the right cast. These were principally country lairds, having no fixed profession, but independent with regard to circumstances.

The most prominent of them, next to my grandfather, who, as senior member, held the situation of president, was one Sir Amalek All-gab, a large portly, broad-shouldered man, with a very simple and good-natured countenance, which, to our boyish eyes, appeared monstrously out of character with his person. Sir Amalek was the last of the line of All-gabs, a family of good repute and cre-

ditable antiquity. We are not informed who was
the first baronet of that name, or upon what occasion the title was conferred. The entailed estate,
however, dependent upon it, was by no means large;
and were not Sir Amalek a bachelor, and in some
respects a thrifty one to boot, the world, that is, all
who knew him, might have reckoned his circumstances to be distressingly narrow. As it was, there
was no reason to form any opinions about the matter; the baronet being a firm adherent to celibacy,
and parsimoniously renouncing a whole catalogue of
small comforts, under the titles of equipage, liveries,
fox-hounds, horses, and champagne.

That Sir Amalek was a doughty angler, no member of the C——h club, save ourselves, ever dis-
puted. He was accustomed to talk them all into a
sort of belief of his prowess; and the strong impression which his narrations made upon our boyish mind,
immediately after our admission into the club, determined us to watch out an early opportunity of
beholding some of these wonderful feats we had
heard vaunted of by the worthy baronet. Right
fortunate we were in pitching upon one among the
very seldom occasions, when Sir Amalek thought
proper to set up his standard of war against the
finny tribes; right fortunate we were in beholding
his huge brawny person, armed with an eight yard
measure, denominated his fishing rod, which (although even to wield it was quite impracticable for

a man of mere ordinary strength) was, to use the baronet's own expression, as a child's whip in his hands; right fortunate, of a truth, we were in beholding him, with a determined air, stride down to the water-edge, draw forth his tackle, and fixing a huge salmon fly at the end of his line, hitch it over the surface of a deep, transparent pool, where, by a certain movement of the angler's wrists, it performed for the space of half a minute a kind of rotatory dance, and was drawn back again to be relieved by a similar insect of more reduced dimensions, whose pas-seul being unable likewise to attract the notice either of trout or salmon, a third such monster was brought forth and introduced upon the self-same stage. All these expedients, however, failing, the baronet betook himself to par-catching, and actually managed to draw in two or three unfortunate wretches, whose butchery seemed to afford mighty satisfaction to their captor, and ended for that day the exploits of the renowned Sir Amalek All-gab. Of course, while spectators of this ludicrous scene, we adopted the precaution of remaining concealed. The presence of a dog overlooking his operations, would have no doubt occasioned a precipitate retreat on the part of this modest angler.

We have made mention of Sir Amalek foremost, not as a specimen of the science and accomplishments under display by the old and long defunct faternity at C———h, but chiefly because he was in some degree looked up to by the club itself as its leading member. He had the talk of three ordinary tongues; and that, combined with his humour, which was infinite, gave him unlimited sway over those with whom he chanced to associate. Even our grandsire, who was wont to exhibit a tolerable proportion of stiff pride, couched a little under the affability of Sir Amalek, and was known more than once to be driven from a favourite position by the torrents of wit and persuasion let loose by the baronet.

Our recollections, however, of these times and matters are very bare, owing to which circumstance, we are compelled to be brief in our delineations of the other members belonging to the old fraternity. The president, our grandsire, bore a striking resemblance, both in feature and character, to his ancestor. As an angler, he excelled not only the rest of the club, but every Borderer and Briton that ever came into competition with him. 'Tis vulgarly rumoured, in the district where he resided, that the fish in a neighbouring stream held holiday on the day of his burial, and testified their exultation by leaping all at once out of the water while his coffin was in the act of being lowered. He died very shortly after his father, aged eighty-one, in consequence of a severe internal contusion, received while out at a black-fishing.

Of the other ancients composing this venerable fraternity, we remember only the names of four.

There was Andy Ged-grapple, laird of the Seggymere Burn, a short, one-eyed, red-faced man, with brains enough to serve a sleeping philosopher. Two things could Andy accomplish; he could catch pike, and drink whisky-toddy, and further he presumed not to attempt.

After him, there was Bauldy Brig-stanes of the Chucky-holm, a sensible, kind-natured, old gentleman, and a keen good angler withal. We ever looked up with great regard to Mr. Brig-stanes, and entertain even to this day a strong respect for his memory. Many were the instructions we derived from him as to the management of our line. Alas! he fell a martyr to his favourite occupation, and was drowned at the age of seventy-one, while attempting, rod in hand, to cross a swollen ford on the Clyde, near Biggar.

Next to the laird of Chucky-holm, we have a faint recollection of one Watty Braw-breeks, brother to the laird of Buskan'-ben. Watty was a sportsman general, and member of all associations from the fraternity at C——h down to the Rat and Badger Club in the ancient town of Hawick. He seldom, however, took his seat with the divan over which my grandfather presided;—its proceedings were not altogether congenial to his unsettled taste, and he seemed to prefer an otter or fox hunt, where all was bustle and activity, to the more solitary employments of our craft. However, we have heard it said, that, when the whim was on him, he generally displayed a knack at getting fish, which occasioned even the president to look wonder-struck. Watty died on his bed, at the good old age of eighty-three; and as he was every-body's man, nobody missed or regretted him.

The last member of the old club our recollection leads us to, and we are often puzzled to comprehend why we have forgotten the others, was Mr. Gilbert Guddle of the Brosy-beck Ha'. Mr. Guddle was a round, squat, bolus-bellied man, with short, thick stumps, and a most brotherly pair of knees;—his phiz was turnip-shaped, and of a pewter colour about the chin. 'Twas a farce to suspect this gentleman of being an angler, and yet he was not without his merits as a killer of fish, although we have heard it hinted that the means he adopted for their destruction were not in all respects the most honest; nor did Mr. Guddle pretend to any secrecy about the matter, but rather prided himself upon his skill in jerking out trout with his hands from under the banks of small streams. The pock-net, too, was a favourite with him, although employed, we suspect, more for the purpose of furnishing a dish for his table (for he possessed an extraordinary and insatiable twist) than of affording him any measure of amusement. Mr. Gilbert, more familiarly termed Gibby of the Beck, was in his way a kind of humorist, and his visage being at all times a droll one, he was enabled, by the smallest contortion of his features, to create a laugh, or, at any rate, to give a very ludicrous effect to all attempts at seriousness on the part of those with whom he happened to be consorted. Mr. Guddle died of apoplexy in the seventy-third year of his age. A most erroneous report was, however, circulated, that being bitten by a water-rat while engaged in ransacking a small burn close to Brosy-beck Ha', he was seized with hydrophobia a few days after. This statement, we aver, upon the authority of his medical attendant, to be totally incorrect.

Such is the amount of all our recollections with regard to the pristine fraternity at C——h. Alas, all its patriarchs have returned to their fathers! Ged-grapple was shot dead by an exciseman, having resisted the seizure of some illegal spirits which he had in his possession ; and Sir Amalek All-gab cleared a road into his coffin by cutting his own throat, which it seems he was not allowed to make unlimited use of during a contested election. As for the other members, having forgotten their names, we have also forgotten their fates. Should there be one alive, from our heart we compassionate him. But why, when old men have no affections like the young—when *their* remembrances are closely sealed up, and ours open afresh, we sometimes know not wherefore—when—how unlike us !—they look upon the world without anxiety, and their fears of parting from it are all time-subdued ? Pity them ! Ay ! nevertheless we do, even because they are so deserted by the glad springs of feeling, because, 'mid their freedom from sorrows, they are deprived alike of their joys.

At the period of our introduction to this assembly of ancients, it was evidently the purpose of our grand-sire, in conjunction with the other wise members belonging to the C——h Angling Club, to provide against the chances of its extinction by drafting into it as many young recruits as they possibly could muster. Accordingly, a week had scarcely elapsed after our admission, when two other candidates were proposed to the fraternity, viz., Messrs. Leister and Otter. These young gentlemen were about the same age as ourselves. They had both completed the ordeal of killing a Tweed salmon, and we believe in a more honest fashion than *we* did.

Before enlarging upon their respective qualities, we find ourselves compelled to take some notice of the singular plan of reinforcement adopted by the old members of the Angling Club. When formed under the direction of our great-grandsire, the fraternity con-sisted of twenty-five members, including the president. To these it seems, by a standing rule, no addition on any account was to be made, and should a vacancy by demise, expulsion, or resignation, occur, it was not to be filled up without the entire consent of the whole remaining members.

It so chanced, that among these primitive brothers of the craft was one Simon Cockle-pate, a self-willed, obstinate, and opinionative bully, whose whole delight

it was to destroy the unanimity of the club, by pre-
venting with his vote, on every occasion, the execution
of its wishes. In vain were appeals made to him by
the various members ; he insisted upon his privilege of
marring their intentions when he thought proper; and
being threatened with expulsion, made use of certain
gestures, which gave the club to understand that his
enmity was by no means to be disregarded. Therefore it was that the peace-loving and irresolute fraternity at C———h made up their minds to endure what
without peril they could not prevent—therefore it was
that their numbers gradually dwindled away, it being
the pleasure of Mr. Cockle-pate to oppose every attempt
to replenish them.

At length, however, after a protracted dictatorship,
this foe to good fellowship walked off the stage of life,
and it was thought necessary, on the part of the club,
to take immediate measures for effecting its own
revival. To introduce, however, a bevy of middle-aged
anglers, even were they able to accomplish such an
object, would be at once to relinquish their own ground,
and change the whole nature of the establishment.
Ancients like themselves they never dreamt of ;—they
designed to give perpetuity to their club; and as a
first step towards the measure, we were hauled in, then
Jack Leister and Tom Otter, all of us mere infants,
just breeched. The lovings of a senile heart, it may be
remarked, are ever with the young. Old men lose regard
for the generation that immediately follows them, and

stretch what remains of their affections towards their children's children.

Of ourselves (we refer to. a period long after the extinction of the old Angling Club at C——h) modesty requires us to say nothing. We could throw a fly, it is true, with some address, and always possessed the art of making our panier appear respectable. Our abilities, however, sunk into insignificance when brought into comparison with the matured skill of our friend Jack Leister. No one could command a line with less effort or better effect. His flies dropped upon the water with most exquisite gentleness. He had a mode of projecting them, when angling below trees, which we never saw practised by any one else. After describing a quarter circle rapidly on either side of him, at a yard's height from the ground, so that he kept free from any intervention of the upper branches, he recovered his line in such a manner, that it proceeded directly from his rod across the stream towards the very spot which he intended it to traverse. We could never thoroughly understand the principle upon which this effect was obtained, no propelling force being employed from behind.

While angling for salmon also, Leister adopted a method, which, without doubt, materially increased the length of his cast. He had a custom of drawing in a considerable portion of the line by means of his hand, and allowing it to dart out

3

with the rest, when in the act of throwing. We have heard him remark that he gained above a fathom of water by this system, but we never had the inclination, or perhaps the necessity, to adopt it ourselves.

The tackle of Jack Leister was of a first-rate description; he prided himself greatly upon his ingenuity in fabricating flies, and he always kept an excellent selection of gut. He likewise made his own rods, and we have seldom handled better wands. The butt-piece was generally constructed of choice fir, and the upper half (for they were of the tie sort, and in two parts only) fashioned of hickory wood. In the grasp, they were light as a riding whip, and so handy, a very infant might brandish them. They managed the line as if it were wild-fire, and, over an impetuous and fresh-run fish, possessed almost incredible power. Their spring was at the same moment strong and facile; they bent to a struggling par, but resumed their arrowy straightness with a tired salmon.

The fly-collection of our friend Leister showed him to be a disciple of the old English school. He was marvellously fond of variety, and sported at least fifty sorts and sizes of insects. The smallest shadow of difference in the wing, dribling, or hackle, was to him of the greatest consequence. He had a mortal aversion to the plain brown palmer, one of the most killing lures we are acquainted with, and his partiality to tinsel was somewhat extravagant. We have seen salmon flies of his which were literally covered with glitter; others, likewise, he fabricated in the Irish style, with a redundancy of the golden pheasant feather under the outer wing, and, to say the truth, they proved in his hands remarkably successful. He once recommended to us a small hook with a light, blue silk body, which he affirmed would prove very deadly on the salmon species in large, clear waters, during the summer months. We never used it, not because we doubted its efficacy, but our experimenting moods are entirely worn off, or, like all anglers, we look upon innovations with a sort of horror.

Leister, when angling, was accustomed to vary his flies every half-hour, and in the case of a salmon refusing the hook, he would run over his whole stock in endeavouring a second time to bring it to the surface. This is not an uncommon practice with some, who, upon raising a fish, have recourse with as much speed as possible to a new and totally different fly. Others, again, recur to the one in use, but refrain from recasting the line until sufficient rest has been allowed to the fish.

Among the members of our modern fraternity, Leister found a powerful rival in the person of Tom Otter. Tom, however, did not equal him as a fly-fisher, but in the management of the minnow was greatly his superior. He had a way of attaching his bait, which gave it a particularly captivating appearance. Under his management, it span with unparalleled activity, and probed into the very haunts of the largest trout. His most eminent feats, indeed, were accomplished with the par-tail, and he gloried not a little in recounting them.

We remember well his description of the capture of a large salmon with this lure. He happened to be trolling in the narrow well-known gorge, immediately below Yair bridge, and while in the act of drawing the bait ashore, he observed behind it a slight convulsion of the water accompanied by one of those momentary gleams, which none but a practised eye can detect as proceeding from the flank of a heavy fish. Tom immediately proceeded several yards higher up the pool, and commenced angling down and across, towards the spot where these indications took place. The salmon again rose, and fortunately, by allowing the bait to run until gorged, he succeeded in hooking it. No sooner was this accomplished, than it commenced its long, steady dart, almost on the surface of the water, terminating it with a sudden plunge, which threatened to snap both rod and tackle. The struggle of the fish to escape proved, however, unsuccessful, and only served to strengthen the hold of its enemy. But still there was no appearance of exhaustion about it. It turned (to use Tom's own expression) like a philosopher, and leisurely walked up the stream, as if meditating upon the three Fates. Suddenly, however it coursed in a new direction, exerting at the same time its whole energies in order to get rid of its tormentor, lashing with its tail at the line, and plunging about with considerable violence. A long rapid run succeeded to these fruitless manœuvres, and Otter had to use his legs to some purpose, in order to save his line, which birred off the reel like a string of lightning. Forthwith the fish once more turned; its broad, huge snout, stemming the upper current, and the tail flapping heavily at intervals; but down again it sunk upon a bed of rock, like a dead, heavy immoveable mass. This was no novel occurrence to Otter; but, as he was not willing to allow the somewhat exhausted fish in any degree to recruit itself, he commenced tossing in large pebbles close to the spot where he judged it lay. In this he was not so speedily successful as he anticipated, for the subtlety of the fish, and per- haps its state of fatigue, retained it at the bottom, in spite of his utmost endeavours to effect a start. At length, however, off it went like a race-horse, making its way along several pools in succession. Otter followed in the rear, at one time immersed waist-deep in the current, at another steering his course close to the margin, under the row of tall, green trees, which overshadow that part of Tweed.

Here, as it happened, he was confronted by a brother angler, engaged like himself with a fast salmon. Unable to control the exertions of his own fish, Tom felt at a loss how to avoid running foul of the long, deep line to which the other struggler was attached. A collision was evident, more especially as the va-

garies of the latter, a newly hooked grilse, prevented
any amicable crossing of rods, such as is generally
adopted on similar occasions.   Besides, the other angler
seemed determined to keep his ground, and preserve
the full altitude of his rod, although Otter's run of line
was considerably the longer.   The spot where this
fellow, a surly poacher from the neighbourhood of
Hawick, happened to stand, was a small ledge of rock
running into a deep, dangerous eddy of water.
Although requested by Otter to alter his position and
lower his rod, both of which he might have done without the slightest risk of losing the fish, he notwithstanding thought proper to remain obstinately immoveable.
Time, however, was not to be thrown aside, the line of
our worthy friend being pretty far spent, and the salmon
in no mood to be thwarted.   Accordingly, enraged at
the hindrance offered by the sulky and determined rustic,
Otter in rather angry terms ordered him a second
time to move out of his way.   This demand not
being complied with, our incensed angler took it at
once into his head to trip up the fellow's heels, in such
a manner that he popped directly into the river,
and commenced floundering for his life in the midst
of the rapid current.   There arose a sort of dilemma
to our friend, who was forthwith called upon to
hesitate betwixt the poacher and the salmon ; and
really, thought he, if to save the one I must relinquish the other, it is no gain to me.   Accordingly, he
continued at his fish, notwithstanding the impre-

cations of the drowning man. These, however, were becoming every moment less vehement. The force of the stream had swept him forwards to a considerable distance, and he was about to sink altogether, when luckily Tom Otter landed his salmon, a thirty pounder, gave it a few smart, killing raps on the head, and hurried to the assistance of the exhausted sufferer. He was not long in rescuing him, the part of the pool to which the poacher had been carried being, although deep, smooth and safe for an expert, venturous swimmer, such as Otter was. The grilse, however, had made its escape, after having broken the line to which it was attached, and the rod likewise of the deserving boor was somewhat injured. Of course, Tom swallowed his curses with excellent humour, bowing profoundly in acknowledgment of the mortified angler's good wishes, and offering him the fins of his huge salmon as a recompence for all loss and damage sustained in his perilous voyage down the Tweed. He then shouldered his fish, and trudged off to another pool, with a snatch of an old ballad in his mouth.

Otter's attachment to Tweedside was altogether uncommon. The river to him seemed hallowed water. He revered its banks and channels, its tributaries, from their very sources, and all belonging to it. With respect to other streams, he was wholly indifferent. He depreciated, above all, the rivers in the north of Scotland, where he happened to sojourn for some months; and although achieving among them several angling feats, he was accustomed to talk of these with great contempt. This was a prejudice on his part, the foundation for which we could never entirely comprehend, as we know of a truth that he was wont to capture most extraordinary loads of fish in a certain Highland water, surpassing by far any that he ever dislodged from the pools of Tweed. But his skill, remarked he, when alluding to his northern campaign, was not put to the test. An urchin unbreeched, without a shred of sagacity, could achieve equal triumphs over the finny tribe, and he was not willing to be reduced to a par with any such.

We check all inclination to marshal off before the reader the various other members composing our late fraternity. Their merits as anglers are unfolded in the records of their communings by the streamside and at the feast table. Why enter into dull details concerning them? They will speak out honestly for themselves. Ah! Doctor, and ye merry-men all—Bill, Tim, Tom, and Harry—have ye fled? Are there to be no more humorous meetings amongst us? Are we defunct indeed? Had we no projects to complete?—no contemplated happinesses yet to enjoy? But be it so! We built up a palace with smoke, and where is it?

# CHAPTER II.

## THE RIVER-SIDE.

### TOM OTTER AND BILL MAY-FLY.

*Otter.* Thou hast an enviable wand, May-fly, and goodly gear; an' thou dost not tempt a fin with these flies of thine, thou art no angler.

*May.* Ay! my rod is a fair one—a neat piece of wood, I must confess; it is light and taper as a water-rush, bends to a breath, but is strong in the marrow as an oak-post; yet, as for my tackle, though it looks tempting, and is wrought seemingly by subtle and fantastic fingers, may I be thrice soused if it will raise even a minnow.

*Otter.* No marvel indeed! thou art whipping at the water like a boatswain's mate, and makest a perfect maelstrom on the surface! Think you that fish will be curious to look at thy flies 'mid such a tempest? Let the line fall more gently, and keep from the edge a pace or two; the best of the pool is where the shadow lies; throw across, and take a curve with thy cast down the stream. That was but a par, and no monster, as thou seemest to think, by that start of thine.

*May.* I pricked him. But ha! did you see that? I have lost both flies; he jerked them off like a pickpocket. What a prime fellow he was!

*Otter.* By no means—only another par; but you struck at him too forcibly. There, you see, he leaps about with your hooks like a ballet-dancer. But arm again, put on this red professor for a trail-fly, and a hare-lug bobber; one of these black hackles will suit as well; you can try either or both, as it pleases you. Be sure to fasten neatly, and tie a firm knot; chop off with your penknife the useless extremities of the gut upon your nail, but not too closely. Now, allow your line to soak a moment at the edge, and set to. I will angle with minnows over the pools already fished. But there! you have got hold of a good trout, a half-pounder at the least. Don't let the line run if you wish to take him, but keep it tight to his mouth, and haul down with the current.

*May.* He is gone also, and bids me good-bye. It provokes one to break his rod, and forswear angling for ever.

*Otter.* Have patience, Bill, have patience; thou must not hope to be a conjuror in the craft all at once. Time will make thee an able hand if thou

perseverest. Keep up heart, my boy, and don't get
into ill-humour with thy flies; they are as pretty
Limericks as I ever set eyes upon, and well barbed
to boot. Only, when thou takest in a good trout,
keep a hand from the line, and allow the rod itself
to do the office, otherwise the fish and you must
part company. Here comes one of our fraternity
—honest Jack Leister, or I mistake—a worthy
angler as ever breathed, and a salmon on his
shoulders. Well, Jack, where got ye that fish?

*Enter* LEISTER.

*Leister.* In the cauldron pool, immediately under the
large cradle-shaped stone, where one who can manage
his fly nicely, may raise a fellow almost every .day of
the year, when the water is in humour. But how,
Otter, are you and May-fly engaged at catching minnows,
and such a prime breeze on the river? Look you, there
is an old, wily trout feeding below yonder bank; my fly
is a salmon one, and would only frighten the rascal; a
grey midge were his surest poison—he would suck it
in eagerly, I warrant you. Lend me your rod, Bill;
this red professor will do the deed notwithstanding.
Now I have him fast! He is a fox of a fish, and
would take himself into cover among the ash roots.
See how he pushes towards the bottom with his strong,
subtle snout, and attempts to saw through his fet-
ters. I must use my bit more powerfully, although
at the risk of losing him. Ha! he feels the barb,

and moves out into deep, unobstructive water ; but he is not nearly exhausted, as you may see by that fling of his.

*May.* 'Tis right vigorous and methodical, and had nigh proved a swamper.    Saw you not how he aimed with his broad tail at the line, or rather threw himself plump upon it, in order to try its strength?

*Leister.* He did so, and might have succeeded in breaking it, had I not been aware of his design, and kept in readiness for it by slackening the reins. But now he confesses himself baffled ; his efforts to escape become weaker ; he turns in three or four directions, and is scarcely able to face the current. I have wheeled his head round, and lead him cautiously along with the stream ; and here he comes to land;—run, Bill, and secure him.

*Otter.* A goodly fish, but somewhat big-pated and black.    I have seen trout more to my fancy ; but this is an old boy, and tough-leathered.

*Leister.* He measures in length about nineteen inches, and weighs short of two pounds.    Ha! look you what the lean, gluttonous cannibal has disgorged !——one of his own species, entire and fresh ; another half-digested ; two small eels ; and a singular concoction of worms, beetles, and leeches.    A hearty meal has he made of them, as you may notice.    Lay him in your creel, May-fly, we shall do likewise in part upon him.    And now, take the trouting-rod, and angle carefully over the next pool ; there be some prowlers out scanning the surface for food. Throw a long, light line, and carry your flies clear of yonder bush, bringing them in on this side of the rapid water, and allowing the trailler to sink a little, while you move them slowly towards you. Strike—there is a fish !

*Otter.* No less than a couple, and both at your beck ; but they are par, small, weak and trashy. Throw them in again, Bill.

*May.* Why so ? Are they not somewhat, and of manifest account ? They will swell the contents of my creel to boot. I will e'en retain them.

*Leister.* As you choose, but do not magnify their dimensions alarmingly, lest the truth creep out in the end. I have known some anglers who turn minnows into whales by the magic of a bounce ; others that have the knack of multiplying one into a dozen, and so forth. It is wiser, however, to be honest in such matters at the first. The braggart, after a stroke or two, is soon detected, and loses generally all his credit at once. Did you ever hear of Rory, the black liar ?

*May.* A strong epithet !

*Leister.* It is a Gaelic one, given to a poor wretch who lives in one of the most miserable of Highland villages in the north of Scotland. This man's mother was a coiner of scandalous stories for the district. Her mouth was eternally foaming falsehoods and exciting mischief. She ruined more reputations with her tongue than an army of cold-blooded villains, giving rise, besides, to petty feuds and disasters without reckoning.   Her darling Rory is a born drunkard, and inherits so strongly his mother's propensities, that all who dwell in the neighbourhood abhor his very presence.   Nature has aptly twisted his shape and features so as to resemble his words. He is the incarnation of falsehood, and yet, strange to say, an angler;—but, mark me, a desperately bad one—the mere murderer of other men's sport.   He rakes and harrows the best pools with nets and other destructive engines, in order to obtain fish, disposing of these as fresh and clean when in their worst and stalest condition.   His braggadocio is staringly large, but too commonplace to be amusing; there are no jokes in the heart of it; it is one concoction and tissue of absolute and unredeemed falsehood.   It has, however, a plot and manner, a minuteness and dramatic progression about it, somewhat imposing.   Rory is too artful not to embellish the deception; he gilds the bolus before he asks you to swallow it.

I once met him, and not at the time knowing my man, was led to ask him concerning some hill lochs which I fancied to exist in the neighbourhood of the village where he lived.   He mentioned the names of several, and of one in particular, where he asserted he had often killed trout of an enormous weight;—more-over, he described its size, situation, and curiosities— gave me an idea of where it lay, and induced me, without much ado, to go in search of it, the distance being a mere trifle, and no guide required.   Off I set, and soon arrived at an eminence from which I was to overlook the promised sheet of water—but where was it? I beheld nothing but a wide stretch of heather, and two or three individuals on its surface cutting moss for fuel. Inquiring of them where the spot lay, they one and all seemed astonished at my query, declared they knew nothing of its existence, and demanded from whom I had received my information. On describing the personal appearance of the man, they broke out into a sort of chuckle, exclaiming, " It was Rory the black liar ! "

*May.* And did you chastise the dog ?

*Leister.* It would need good leather to take skin from the devil ! But, look you, what a lovely trout Tom Otter is in the act of landing.

*Otter.* I have him hooked with my minnow-tackle, and in such a prime stream, no wonder the fish is a good one ; see what a breadth he has, and how unlike the large-headed monster captured a few minutes ago. He wants five inches of its length, and weighs notwithstanding an additional half-pound. He is in miniature what I once took in Loch ———— ; but I must get him paired speedily from the same pool, and with a fresh bait. Choose me a minnow, May-fly, out of the pitcher.

*May.* Here is a large one, and coloured like a rainbow.

*Otter.* Toss it away ! Thou art no judge of a dainty bait. I want a small, silvery, spruce-look-

ing fellow, with a lively eye, and smooth forehead.

*May.* I have fingered out the very imp;—but he
is slippery as a pig's-tail, and has fallen somewhere
among the grass.   Ha! here he is, dancing about
with the spirit of a mountebank.

*Otter.* I have fastened him to my wish, and he
turns admirably.   I saw a fish follow to the water's
edge; and there again! the same sly prowler;—but
he has seen me, and slinks off.   Heaven forgive him!

*Leister.* He was no doubt a thunderer, Tom, his
escape annoys you so terribly.

*Otter.* And well it might; for a goodlier trout never
showed fin, even to old Isaac himself; no, nor in-
habits black Styx, nor Lethe, with its laudanum-
running streams;—but he shall die to-night!   His
haunt is under that tuft of rushes, and a par-tail will
spring him an hour or so after sunset, else the skill is
out of Otter's right hand.

*May.* Bravo! thou art a threatful and dangerous
man, and wilt extirpate the whole race of giants.
Methinks I espy Timothy Gaff wending down the hill
to join us.

*Leister.* Thou art right, Bill; and who are with
him but our skeleton-shaped friend, Harry Hackle,
and worthy Doctor Swiveltop!   Are they not angling dons of the first-water, tastefully rigged out
in modish apparel?   Yet Harry is a genuine
sportsman, and throws a fly with wonderful neat-

ness and precision. The Doctor himself is no bad
hand at the par-tail and minnow, but prides himself
over-much upon his novel contrivances in the way of
tackle. He angles upon a system, and his system is
not exactly the true one ; for it seldom manages the
capture of above half-a-dozen good trout, and a couple of
small pike. Gaff is, without question, the best angler
of the three ; that is to say, he kills more fish in the
same space of time than either, or perhaps both, of the
others. There is nothing, however, extraordinary in
his manner of going to work. The secret of his success lies in his being able at a glance to discern the
best water ;—he seldom flings away a throw ; but
angles a good deal too rapidly for my taste, striding on
before one, and picking up the choicest fish without
stay or compunction.

*May.* We can bind him to a tree, should he intend
the same trick at present.

*Otter.* Fortunately, he is without rod, and must act
the mere spectator of our exploits, which are not likely
to be wonderful, seeing that the breeze is low and the
sun strong.—But how fares it with our gallant friends,
Harry Hackle, Timothy Gaff, and Doctor Nathan
Swiveltop ?

*Enter* GAFF, HACKLE, *and* SWIVELTOP.

*Hackle.* Right heartily. We are fresh from the
city, and armed at all points with health and humour. Are fish astir to-day, and what wonders
have been enacted among them ? You have killed

4

an angel of a salmon, Leister ;—he weighs nine pounds at the least, and is broad, thick, and clean-run. Some of these trout are to be talked of reverently, and ought to have given glorious sport. We must lie upon our oars until to-morrow, and then——

*May.* An ominous and prophetic pause! By the ghost of old Isaac! Hackle, you intend to level us into mere nothings—to take the conceit out of us in a twinkling; but no, old boy!

*Hackle.* Ah! Bill, we had almost forgotten thee. Thou art the newest top-piece of our divining rod, and mayest, in a season or twain, work miracles ; at present go catch gudgeons; thy cunning may achieve thus far. They are a silly, quickly-gulled manner of fish ; a thread and crooked pin may fill thee a hatful.

*May.* Were it thy hat, Hackle, the wisdom I should drop into it were weightier than it has contained hitherto. But, seeing thou fanciest thyself to have some trouting wit, I am willing to back Leister against thee for three songs and a supper, to be paid nightly to all present after each successive combat, during our stay.

*Hackle.* Not agreed to, Bill.—Fortune is no friend of mine.

*May.* This salmon afears thee, Hackle ; thou hast a doubt of thyself more than of Fortune. We shall have our song and supper notwithstanding. What say you, Timothy ?

*Gaff.* So be it, Bill. But this meadow is sweet and fragrant. What hinders us, now that the air is hot and the fish dull, to seat ourselves awhile on the grass ? Hollo ! Doctor, thou must keep to our company, and not probe the water against all usage. There is nothing to be made out of it at present.

*Swivel.* Indeed, sagacious sir ! This nibble refutes thee at the outset; look, what a masterly tug ! and there again ! my line is forced out. I have him.

*Gaff.* An eel, Doctor. Ha ! ha !

*Swivel.* No bad fish, Master Timothy; nay, the very pick of dainties to those who are men of discernment.

*Gaff.* Such as thyself, for instance. But the ugly rascal has gorged thy hook to his centre; bisect him if thou art wise, and uprip his catacombs.

*Swivel.* As you say, Tim; we shall unfold our lancets, and lay on among his vitals.

*Gaff.* His vitals, Doctor—the vitals of an eel ! Thou must needs shred him into morsels ere thou findest them.

*Leister.* Barbarous and inhuman talk ! unworthy of anglers and of a refined age ! Gaff and Swiveltop, you are twain unnaturally savage souls. Dash at once the poor, lingering reptile against the ground ; it will put an end to its sufferings, and save us the pain of listening to your abhorrent and damnable schemes.

*Swivel.* O rare sentimentalist ! Know you not that eels are heretics, and we the inquisition ? But

your counsel shall be followed to the letter. See
what a lovely paralysis it has effected; the creature is
stone dead; and now I shall creel him up for burial,
and join your group. Ha! Hackle! you are sketching.
A cottage, a tree, a hill, and a river,—all indispensable
objects in a taking landscape.

*Hackle.* Moreover, I shall not forget Doctor Swiveltop in the foreground butchering eels; it will finely
relieve the other ingredients of the scene, and add
wonderfully to its general effect.

*Otter.* You say justly; the Doctor's person would
help to dignify the subject; and yet, in sooth, there
is much to admire on all sides of us. Yon group of
elms might be chosen as the bath-guardians of Diana,
they are so leafy and patriarchal. What stems several
of them possess! gnarled and warted over from the
root upward; their shadows too are entirely pagan.
One could imagine Night herself to issue out, like a
vampire, from under those solemn hangings. No pencil
can do them justice. They defy, with their brandished
arms, all the trickery of art.

*Hackle.* 'Tis a venerable group, but heavy, umbra-
geous, and too closely massed for pencil-work; it wants
meaning and variety, and resembles a square thunder-
cloud. I dislike it uncommonly, and would rather yon
solitary and disfigured oak, blast-worn and thin-
mantled as it is—a forest-outcast, cleft athwart the
chest—its muscles, aye, its heart laid bare, but still
existing—existing as if in the teeth of nature.

*Otter.* Perhaps you are right, but you judge only with the pictorial eye. I am taken with both, and admire each the more for the contrast's sake. It is so also in regard to those hills. One is huge and uniform, coated with heath and verdure ; knolls, pleasant, pastoral, and sunny, scattered over it ; its summit round, smooth, and shining ; its base thick and sovereign-like. The other is a mere rock, of more contracted dimensions ; but still vast, having the forehead of a Gorgon ; scarred with ravines ; and on its side, a torrent of shivered granites, arrested singularly in their descent. Altogether, indeed, it is a motley but pleasant scene.

*Hackle.* It is so, and under skilful hands might form a lovely sketch. This river is the spirit of the picture ; it glides into it and out of it with a dream-like imperceptibility ; here sunned and sparkling, there shaded and sombre. I admire much the long, still, shadowy pool, situated under yonder cliff, on which you may discern the grey and ivied battlements of a feudal castle.

*Otter.* I have killed ofttimes a good salmon at the upper part of it, where there are two or three choice eddies, and a delectable stream. At this moment I perceive two fishers, not of the worthiest sort, busily employed in harrowing it with the double rod.

*Leister.* Let us up and put an end to their sport, if this nefarious manner of angling can so be termed.

*Gaff.* You advise well. They deserve a severe

drubbing, and a bellyful besides of river water ; at any rate, we shall give them a screed of our opinion, and compel their compliance into the bargain.

*May.* Nay, now, we had better delay our interference ; it will gain us nothing but ill-will and a grudge. These rascals never forgive what they imagine to be an insult, and are in no wise particular about the manner of their revenge. What say you, Doctor ?

*Swivel.* Why, stand up for our rights, to be sure. —Can we hit upon a better plan than to march up at once in two bodies to their shoe points, and, without even a good-morrow, commence stretching a series of cross-lines in front of them ? It nettles a man stylishly to be foiled with his own weapon !

*Leister.* Good, Doctor ; the expedient is an admirable one. Hackle, yourself, and I, will ford the river ; while Otter, May-fly, and Tim Gaff, assail them on this side of it.

*Swivel.* Moreover, let us hang out instead of tackle an array of scares, in the shape of crow-feathers ; they are to be found, I have no doubt, in great plenty under yonder rookery in the elm-grove.

*Otter.* Excellent, Doctor ; thou hast the knack of scheming well ; so we shall e'en lend thee a hand, in order to take the devil destructive out of these rascals.

# CHAPTER III.

ANOTHER PART OF THE RIVER.

*Enter* TWO POACHERS.

*1st Poacher.* Haud up your wand a bit, Watty; ye're playin' the deil wi' us a'thegither. What gars ye wark the flees in that fashion?

*2d Poacher.* Faith! man, it's no sae easy managin' them as ye think; there's a muckle troot on the near end o' the line.

*1st Poacher.* Tak him in, then, an' dinna spoil the lave o' the water; there's twa fathom to ye, and be canny. Gie these bits o' par a yerk into your creel, and fasten on a hantle sawmon flees;—there's a gude chance o' a fish amang thae rocks. It was just here we hookit the thirty punder last Martinmas. Ye'll mind hoo it bang up wi' its muckle head to the yellow flee, and awa, when it fand itsel' grippit, to yon stane, and there it lay, like a clod,

as if it hadna sense or motion, till we stirred it up wi'
a ring o' hard airn, and doon again it darted, amaist on
the tap o' the water, its braid tail stickin' oot ahint,
an' noo and then giein' a sair and wrathfu' wallop!
There's the very spot whare we landed the cratur;
an' no easy wark, as ye ken, it was; for I had lost the
handle o' my gaff, and couldna get Jock Anison to
strike the huik intil it, as he micht hae dune. We
made a famous catch o't that day, forbye what the twa
grilses fetched—Sax-and-twenty shillings, hard money,
atween the pair o' us! But what gran' callants are
these haudin' up in this direction? I wish they
mayna spoil our water amang them.

*2d Poacher.* The deil's in the chaps, wi' their
strings o' craw-feathers, and ither sic nonsense!
They're gane clean witless. Hollo you! what gars
ye hinder ither folk's sport in siccan a fashion? Is
this like respectable gentry, to gang direct up to the
very front o' twa honest men, an' commence fricht-
ening the fish frae their presence? Awa wi' ye,
gin ye be wise, an' dinna brak the temper o' Wat
Waddell.

*Enter* LEISTER, OTTER, MAY-FLY, SWIVELTOP, HACKLE, *and* GAFF,
*on either side of the river.*

*Swivel.* Fish rise well, gentlemen—crow's feather
capital! Strike, Tim! What a huge fellow! a
sturgeon! Ha! you missed him; never mind.
There again—a mere minnikin. Shake him off,

Tim; that's good. Hurra! a mermaid! Give line, Tim. Softly, boy, softly, lest you tear the lip vermilion, and mutilate the peachy complexion. What a rare creature she is! How she astonishes these natives behind us with her languishing sky-blue eyes, and light amber hair! By the shade of Tobit! we shall capture her, and feasten therewith the palate of regal epicures! Ha! saw you that bosom with its twain huge semi-pearls? How it rose up luringly from the pool, and then vanished? Again! —and such a face of sorrow and superhuman anger I never beheld. Her tresses are all dishevelled, her features mangled; and now, she dives down to her rocks of coral, and, lute in hand, performs her death-dirge. Hold tight, Tim, and keep her head down with the stream.

*Hackle.* Good, Doctor; the achievement is wonderful. There is witchcraft in these crow-feathers of yours—most astonishing! Let this honest man have a peep at your tackle. We may entrust him with the secret.

*Swivel.* Not for worlds! I pray thee, keep the clown at a distance. It becomes us not to countenance his curiosity. Who or what is he, that the renowned inventor of the mermaid-fly should succumb to instruct him? Were he a brother of the craft, like thyself, honest Hackle, one might be reduced to tolerate his intrusion. But not so, my ancient chum; he wants the distinctionary characteristics of our worthy fraternity. *He* is a base, bungling water-raker, and no angler.

*2d Poacher.* I'd gie a croon-piece for a grip o' ane o' your throttles, ye senseless pewter-heids. What richt hae you, I ax, to stap in afore ane, and steir up the pride o' the water wi' your nonsense in this wise? It's a shame till ye to be plaguin' the like o' us; and ye'll repent it, I'se warrant ye!

*Hackle.* Thou art bold, friend, and somewhat saucy; see you not we are double-rod fishers, like thyself—fair dealers after a kind. Come, let thy wrath cool, and be wise;—shut up the sluice-gates of revenge, else shall we spare thee a ducking. Nay, now, look not to thy fellow across the river; there be enough at his elbow to keep him in trim;— and mind, when angling in future, you leave some chance of success to those behind you.

*Leister.* This is like preaching to the devil, Hackle;—but the rascals slink off to perpetrate their iniquities somewhere else. Well do I recollect the physiognomy of one of them. He is an arrant desperado — a natural mischief-maker. His respect for the game-laws is like that of a buzzard-hawk. A grey-hen on her eggs is not safe in his presence. He would unshell the very chicks, in order to satiate his sanguinary lust! I have seen him with a pannier-full of birds slung across his shoulders, none of them feather-soiled, but all noosed and netted from the choicest coppices and corn-

fields of the district.    He has the various calls by rote
and instinct, and can lure, almost to his arm's-reach, a
harem of moor-hens.    He is the pink and paramount
of poachers—an apt and dead shot—a tasteful dog-
breaker, sinewed like the hill-fox, with somewhat also
of its sneaking and cowardly dispositions.    When
challenged, he exhibits his gun in such a manner as
effectually to keep at bay the individual attempting to
capture him.    How he has managed so long to escape
the handcuffs, is to me a matter of wonder; for the
villain would halt at nothing, and has no more compunction or sensibility than a tiger-cat.    In fact, without allowing an over-sufficiency of credit, I have reason
to give some faith to the report of certain sable
delinquencies, which, if committed by him, display in
its true colours the vindictive nature of the vagabond.

*Swivel.* There is a prank in his pate at present,
or I much mistake.    See you, he fords the water,
in order to join his vinegar-visaged companion.
That the twain are holding war-council, you may
divine from their gestures.    Let us cross also, and
increase our forces on the opposite bank.    Two such
able-bodied scoundrels might drub the breath out
of them ere our column come into action.

*Leister.* No fear.    They will fight it stoutly;
and yet, to keep off mischief, we may as well be at
hand.    Such vagabonds are in nowise particular
about their mode of attack, and will not hesitate to
use sturdier weapons than their mere fists.

*Swivel.* As you say; the knobs metallic of these ponderous clogs of theirs might fell a buffalo. I had rather be pawed upon with the hoof of a mettlesome stallion than risk my bones so unsatisfactorily. The dogs are giving signals to some one. Hollo, Otter! keep a look-out to the right. There is need of a sharp eye.

*Otter.* And no lack of one, Doctor. I take the heart out of your hint.

*Hackle.* Methinks these ugly customers are well backed, however; there be no less than five or six others advancing to join them. Such a band of rag-gamuffins!—Satan-visaged rascals!—They would make the tread-mill go round merrily.

*Swivel.* One hath a cock in his eye, and is sinister as a lean raven; another hath the shoulders of a Milo, and sports a pair of huge Erebean whiskers: he is the don of the crew, and in time of desperation might wrench off a man's head with his mouth. I marvel how he manages to find food for such a magnificent semi-globe.

*Leister.* A pennyworth would preserve him. Being an exciseman, he subsists entirely by drink.

*Swivel.* An exciseman — and a poacher — and a drunkard!

*Leister.* Ay, Doctor! Thou art not lessoned in these matters. Thou knowest little of the excise in Scotland. It has proved the curse and canker-worm of our country: its influences have deranged

the entire community. Instead of promoting social
order and happiness, or of furthering the cause of
virtue, they have only served to create misery and oppression, and withal to encourage the increase of crime.
Our Elysian soil, from which root to root, morality and
religion were wont to spring, has been impregnated,
out of the storehold of this baneful system, with the
seeds of contention, profligacy, and harm! Who, in
fact, are most of the dirty-jobbers employed in its
service, but a set of worthless miscreants, and reduced
debauchees—men, of course, who have few pretensions
to principle, and fewer still to those golden charities
of the heart, those tendrils of our natural philanthropy,
which have adorned the virtuous in all ages? What
such creatures effect in the way of contaminating
an unguarded people is almost incredible. Disposed
of in an artificial manner through every item in the
land, they enforce their several examples beyond the
reach of control. Achieving nothing but corruption
of principle, and the unfrequent demolition of a few
whisky stills, they are incomed, notwithstanding, with
large and lavish emoluments. The public gain nothing
but detriment at their hands; and yet the public it is
by whom they are pampered up. Every one knows
how the poet Burns felt his situation among them—
how he abhorred the company necessity had compelled
him to mingle with! Since his time, they have
grown worse and worse, and, strange to say, although
cursed by him from his very heart, glory in the fact

that he was forced to be one of themselves. Forced he was, indeed! To select, willingly, the outcast bread of an exciseman, is to abandon for ever all principle, all feeling, and all hopes of redemption to come!

*Swivel.* This is a tirade, Jack—a right impetuous volley of words! But see these worthies are charging down upon our comrades; we must ford the stream and unite forces.

*Exeunt.*

---

### ANOTHER PART OF THE RIVER.

*Enter* LEISTER, OTTER, MAY-FLY, *&c., &c. ; also* POACHERS.

*Gaff.* They love not our appearance, methinks, and will move off after all.

*May.* I trust not. Let us force the shy humour out of them should they flinch. Are they not more in number than we are, abler-bodied, and stronger-sinewed, having fists like rough iron cased in harness-leather? Why then not encounter us? Ha! they advance like men and heroes! How now? What need ye, my honest fellows, that ye beat up our intrenchments so unceremoniously? Are ye on a pilgrimage, and want food? Are ye traffickers, and have wares to dispose of? Foot-pads haply? Nay, look not so wisely ignorant, so lost-like. Maybe we can aid you in your perplexity. Come, be talkative; unlock your jaw-bones, and let run the reels of your discourse.

*1st Poacher.* We'll tak the jaw oot o' you first, Maister Muckle-gab. There's naethin' like a richt lesson for you gentry. Sae haud till them, Wat, and let them ken it.

*2d Poacher.* That we will, there's nae mistakin'. Come on, chaps.

*3d Poacher.* Losh! sic a clooter as I hae gotten frae this lang chiel! It has amaist dang in the neb o' me! His neive's like a perfect sledge-hammer. I canna stand till't ony langer.

*1st Poacher.* Ye're no gaun to cut, Rab, ye white-livered loon? Back, if ye're wise, or ye needna peril a sicht o' your shadow for thae three twalmonths. Wat, man, can ye no tak' the spunk oot o' that sma' weasel-lookin' callant?

*2d Poacher.* Faith, Jock, its kittlish wark gettin' a grip o' him; he's like the tail o' a moss-ether, gye an ill to haud, forbye the stang. Deil tak him! if the varmint hasna driven twa o' my foreteeth doon my thrapple. It's waesome to part wi' sic auld freends.

*1st Poacher.* Get his head doon aneath your oxter, and lay it intill him like the very mischief.

*2d Poacher.* Easier said than dune; it's ill seein' through a patch o' blue waifers; my barrel ee's naethin' better at present. But what's the gauger aboot?

*1st Poacher.* Ax himsel; he seems hard put to't.
The four half mutchkins hae spoilt him a'thegither.
There's a muckle chap there has got him clear under,
and he's no sma' beer.

*4th Poacher.* It's time for us to be aff, callants! I'm
a' a clod o' sairs. They're no canny customers thae
gentry.

*2d Poacher.* Geordie's in the richt; it's nae fun
gettin' lickit like a wheen bairns. Tak to your legs,
Jock, an' leeve the exceeseman; he's no worth a bodle
at rinnin'!

*Exeunt* POACHERS.

*Swivel.* Nobly done, my hearties! We've doctored
them in style, my river militia-men! But what
carcass is this on the field?—The black-whiskered
gauger, I declare. Vulnerable after all, old boy?
Are there cracks and fissures in the hide of such a
rhinoceros? How he grunts, like the mandarin of a
boar-stye! We must pommel him up again; he is only
semi-thrashed, and can spare half a stone additional
of ruby blood. Run, May-fly, and fetch a capful of
river water; there is no restorative like a good
sousing!

*May.* Beyond all compare, it is the best of soberers,
if largely administered. Methinks I espy a tub not
far from this, belonging to some washerwoman, which
should answer dashingly. Gaff and I will run for it.

*Exeunt* GAFF *and* MAY-FLY.

*Swivel.* Do so.   And how reckon we our wounds, comrades, after this desperate affair ?   Any maladvertences or sanguinary effusions ?—any dental infractions or dislocations of the ossa ?—the nasal arches uninjured, and no tendons divided ?   Thou hast a curtain on thy left eye, Leister, I note ;—and ho ! Harry Hackle, thou art lame as a modern hexameter ; —and thou, Tom Otter !—But there is nothing like it, boys.

*Hackle.* Amen, Doctor !   We have come off swimmingly ; save the hoof-mark of that drunken behemoth, I am skatheless as ever.   It were better to be maimed outright with an oaken cudgel, than have such a monstrous piece of ordnance as a gauger's leg driven athwart our shins !

*Swivel.* Revenge, Harry, acts as a sweet salve. Here come Gaff and May-fly to retaliate for thee. We will of a truth cool the dog's forehead with this surcharge of the element ; and, O ye tritons and river-amphitrites, bear a hand !   How cozily the rascal lies ; his huge bluster-ball of a skull half sunk in moss.   He hath a touch of the Russian autocrat in his countenance.   'Tis a pity he is not a tyrant, and we patriots—how neatly we could massacre him !

*Leister.* Shame, Doctor ; you have not the heart of a Turk.

*Swivel.* Towards this excise-bear, that I have, Jack.   We shall jerk off our thunder-plump athwart

5

his muzzle.   Bring the pitcher to this side, and be ready to start, boys.—Now for it !

> SWIVELTOP *and* MAY-FLY *empty the water tub on the* GAUGER.

*Exciseman.*   Ugh !—d—n it !—What the mischief's here ?—blast them !—Wat, Rab, ye deil's taed-eaters !—whar hae ye gane, ye gude for nae-things ?   Ugh ! Ye'll get it, as shure's I'm a born man.—Ugh ! ugh !

> *Exeunt.*

———

### ANOTHER PART OF THE RIVER.

*Enter* LEISTER *and* OTTER.

*Otter.*   The evening is a delicious one.   How lightly across our favourite pool steals the dew-winged zephyr! The late shower seems just to have ambered the water, and no more.   It is in the loveliest of trims.   Not a trout keeps its shelter, save two or three of the largest, and these also will soon be astir after their food.   I prefer much the arching boughs of this oak-tree to the coffin of a room we have just left, with all its roaring jollity and good-fellowship.

*Leister.*   Ay, Tom, 'tis the winning side of the

contrast, and so would even our friend, the Doctor, allow, could we have prevailed upon him to quit his close quarters for the fresh, kind air of heaven, the fading landscape, and another bout at the river.    But let us put our tackle in readiness.    I have an eye after that calm, deep bend, a short way before us, and shall first give it a trial with small moth flies, and, when it becomes darker, use my famous black beetle.

*Otter.*    Your famous black beetle, Jack !—Let me see it.

*Leister.*    Here it is : merely a large ebon hackle twisted round a strong hook, and winged with raven feather.

*Otter.*    As you say.    But, I presume, you find it killing on occasions ?

*Leister.*    Always—during calm summer nights.    It takes the cunning out of an old trout amazingly. These small moth-hooks are poor killers in comparison. However, as it is still twilight, I shall give them the prior chance.    You intend to confine yourself to the minnow ?

*Otter.*    I do ; and a dozen of the sweetest, silvery-sided little spinners have I gotten.    They will be the death of an equal number of goodly trout, or I mistake my skill.    Look you how transcendently this one is baited ; it will run to perfection.

*Leister.*    These water-coots destroy one's patience ; what a lovely cast this had been, were it not broken up by the flight of that bird.    I noticed a large trout feeding on the way of its trail, and now it has retired to the bottom, and probably will not rise again for some time.    There goes another of the plagues!    I wish it were in a pike's mouth, or had an ounce of lead under its wing.    Bats, too!    One might suppose himself angling in Lake Avernus, with a cloudful of hobgoblins on each side of him!    These leather-winged imps are wonderfully taken with my line and flies.    I have caught one of them! a curious little creature, having the face of a virtuoso or relic-gatherer, with a spark or two of more sagacity about him.    He has swallowed the hook, and as I cannot extricate it easily, must needs put an end to his sufferings by placing my foot upon him.

*Otter.* 'Tis a pity to do so, and not rather set him at large.    Such a small piece of wire may work no harm to his vitals, should you allow it to remain.    Divide the gut close to his teeth.    There he goes, straight to the old oak-tree where his lodge is, in the caverned arm-pit of a shadowy bough——

*Leister.* To die of indigestion.    But see, Tom, a trout followed your minnow to the surface; you might have fixed him too, had your eyes been where they ought, and your swivels in motion.

*Otter.* Perhaps he will thrust at it again; hunger gives courage to some creatures.    Am I not right?    I have him beautifully bridled, and will lead him round this alder bush into a cove or bay.    Seize him, Jack, with your hand, and let him smell our atmosphere. Hold! he is too strong yet, and may escape.

*Leister.* I have my fingers round his body, like so many lassoes, and a plump handful he is. But it is now dark enough for my beetle fly; and there are` three tempting holes not far off, where I intend to dip it. One of them is quite palace-ground for a kingly fish! There is a sort of still eddy in it, and, on the near side, a gathering of white froth, stretching to the bank itself. Under this lies a man's depth and more of water, at the bottom of which are several old trunks and tree-roots, full of fissures and hiding-places. I have frequently seen the lips of a goodly fly-sucker kissing the surface thereabout, and hope to tempt him towards me ere long. The hero is on the feed at this moment—you may notice his air-bell scattered up and down. I have hold of him, Tom!—egad, I have. He is a noble fish, and would run a cable.

*Otter.* Bravo! Jack, be sparing of your line, not-withstanding. These dead roots, should they catch, will play the mischief with it. He makes for them to a certainty. Show him the strength of your tackle; you may do so without dread of its giving way. Now he turns, and takes a cruise towards the opposite bank. Humour him, and allow the reel to move more readily; —again, work your windlass, and haul in.

*Leister.* He is scarcely exhausted, and still keeps on the poise; but I have the upper hand of him beyond doubt, and can teach him the four cardinal points with a few twists of my arm. You see now how submissively he comes to land, and turns his broad, starry-side uppermost upon the channel. Four pounds and a half is his weight, barring three ounces, and a lovelier trout seldom kissed the shore.

*Otter.* We must have him at supper an hour hence. That black beetle of yours, Leister, is a witch! I have twirled a minnow over this hole fifty times, and not shaken a single fin. It will be long ere it get another such resident as this! What an ogre the fellow must have been to travelling par and the young wanderers of its own species! How startled they would be when he dashed after them, with his grim jaws horribly expanded! Methinks I behold the swarms floundering on these shallows opposite, earnest to escape from the inexorable cannibal. It is not a straggler he seizes, but the plumpest and foremost of the shoal—a nimble, silver-sided water-pet, which one would have imagined could beat him hollow in the chase.—But my rod is idle, and time flies. I shall only beat down this pool with my minnow, and give over.

*Leister.* It is almost time to do so. This dew is falling to some purpose, and I have no wish to be drenched altogether. What animal is that moving among these rushes? You hear it, Tom?

*Otter.* Ay, Jack; it is an otter, or I mistake. He is at some distance from the water, and had we cudgels and were active enough, we might intercept his retreat, and add the marauder to our spoils.

*Leister.* There is no want of weapons; let us wrench up a couple of stakes out of this old paling and set upon him. I have a spear on the butt-end of my rod, which might pierce the corslet of a rhinoceros.

*Otter.* Hist! He will notice us, and contrive to escape. Steal you softly with me along the margin of the river, so as to be able to rush directly up towards the spot where we now perceive him. He is occupied, methinks, with the carcase of a large salmon or pike; and, if we act cautiously, will not suspect our approach until fairly attacked. Deal your bitterest blows upon his pate, and give no quarter.—This way, Jack.

*Leister.* The fellow defends himself like a hero, and would fain have a hold of my leg. Beshrew me! if he hasn't chopped this cudgel in style. Those teeth of his might champ iron, and I had as lief have it mutilated under the spokes of a mill-wheel as trust a limb of mine within his jaw-vice. You hit him cleverly, Tom, and have fractured his helmet.

*Otter.* So methinks, the creature sprawls like a riddled Frenchman! Another tap, gently dealt, will demolish him.

*Leister.* He is dead as his grandsire of the ark! Saw you ever so stuffed and oily a carcass?—such a bon-vivant of a brute? He hath a touch of the alderman under his jacket—a blown, pulpy, and dropsical aspect about him, that renders it more the marvel how he could display such activity, and suffer so many hard licks as he did. Well the glutton knew what are the choicest morsels on a clean-run salmon! Look you how this noble fish has been dealt with! All the epicure bits torn scientifically out. What a gap there is betwixt the pectoral and ventral fin, and round the shoulders also!—See what gobs have been extracted!

*Otter.* Ay, Jack, well may all honest anglers applaud us for the service we have done them in destroying this river-tyrant and unconscionable glutton! But we must bind his legs together, and carry him shoulder-high over one of these stakes; he will astonish bravely our fraternity at the inn, and extract a fling of ecstacy from the worthy Doctor. It is high time for us to march, and we are laden, like kings, triumphant.

*Exeunt.*

# CHAPTER IV.

## ROOM IN THE INN.

### MAY-FLY, SWIVELTOP, GAFF, *and* HACKLE.

*Swivel.* 'Tis a craze, Bill, a very craze, this out-of-door humour of Otter's and Jack Leister.—I abhor night angling! 'Tis a chill, comfortless business, suited to savage likings and the blood of brutes. How much more befitting is it, and congenial to our natures, to mete out the evening together in · social converse, coloured and improved by the influences of the circling toddy jug!

*May.* As you say, Doctor. I envy not, nor yet greatly compassionate them; they will capture only an ague-touch or dew-fever. No trout itself would venture abroad at hours so unseasonable as this! 'Tis a craze altogether, as you say.

*Swivel.* Ay! Bill, truly so. Fill up your glasses, my boys—there is no peril in this good liquor! I

hate all moping and owlishness, and measure my attach-
ments according to the latitude of a Christian countenance.    Come,   take   a   provoker   to   mirth,  honest
Timothy ;   and   thou,  Hackle,  is  thy  palate  out  of
humour,  man,   or   hath   the   sober   fit  seized  thee ?
Drink !  Bah !  this  world  will  run  to  wreck  for  sheer
want  of  jollity !   'Tis  fancied  becoming,  now-a-days,
to wear the visage of a death's-head, and look apostolic-
ally demure and Santon-like—to whine and grunt over
God's mercies, and use weak water to deluge  our  wits
withal !   Some  men  seem  born  only  to  see  their  coffins
made,  and  deal  ice  among  their  fellows.   We  have
none  of  the  rare,  old,  Bacchanal  souls  among  us—the
prime  wits  of  three  gone  centuries !   Alas, no !  they
are  run  out  and  become  extinct.   Where  is  the  twinkling  humour  of  the  eye,  that  we  remember  our  grand-
fathers  to  have  had—the  right  comic  setting  of  the
mouth,  and  puckering  of  the  cheeks ?—Where  is  the
tongue  always  agog—the  droll  gait  and  gesture—the
endless  fund  and  wallet-store  of  rich  and  racy  anecdote,  snatch  and  stave,  jest  and  merriment ?   Oh !
your  modern  men  do  and  dare  nothing !   They  can
mimic  no  better  than  elephants,  and  when  they
laugh, 'tis  after  the  fashion  of  hyenas ;—they  white-
wash  their  faces,  deeming  it  sage-like  to  look  pale
and  spectral ;  they  are  cold,  cautious,  narrow,  and
knavish—full  of  glooms,  frets  and  heart-aches,  galled
livers  and  consumptions.   Out  on  them  that  cannot
find  flowers  and  honey  on  the  field  of  life,  but  must

needs exhume its bitter roots, wherewith to feed their melancholy!

*Hackle.* Your satire, Doctor, is wickedly over-charged : There be fires and faces merry as ever, in our free, glad homes—hearts light and innocent, that need not the goading impulse of strong drinks in order to stir them up—that call not to aid the blands of novelty, but are alway buoyant, alway in time to joyous measures.

*Swivel.* I know it, Hackle ; but over their cups men are no hypocrites. See the wariest of them reveal themselves ; they betray their characters, and open up their schemes ; they let out the issues of frail human-ity ! Here it was that Shakspeare took lessons in the study of mankind ; here true philosophy is taught, and not in abstract spheres, in grave, solemn circles, nor in wildernesses, nor in garrets. Over the cup, my boys, more glorious things have been uttered than are written in immortal books ; the walls of the senate-house have been put to shame by the eloquence displayed in corners at the feast-table ! Yet, mark me, Hackle, I cry not up the drunkard who extinguishes reason ; I cry not up that excessive indulgence, which takes the curb off our passions, and allows an impress to the dominant powers of darkness ;—moderation, boys, moderation in all things !

*May.* Eh ! Doctor, and thyself as the example, most abstemious Swiveltop ? By the bye, Gaff yonder is sound asleep, and there is some inclination to nod in my own brain-holder. We must be early astir to-morrow, in order to have anything like sport. I intend starting for the river about sunrise.

*Swivel.* One might suppose, Bill, from the way you talk, that you were really an angler, instead of which you can manage your rod no better than a tailor's needle. Come, recount thy feats, give us the pick of thy miracles, that we may canonize thee ! Preach of thy ten-pounders and thirty-pounders—thy *salmones feroces, erioces et truttæ*—thy silver-edged hackles, and green gooseberry ephemeræ—thy genuine O'Shaughnessys and taper Chevaliers—thy complex multipliers and witch-hair casting lines—thy baits and surfeit-worms, red coral roe, and pearl minnows ; be large in thy discourse, and learned withal, as if the matter were well digested and intimate to thee ; make thy notes, strictures, and digressions ; muster up thy forces, Bill, and tilt at all usage and observance.

*May.* O facetious Swiveltop ! thou art the king of wits ; thy tongue waggeth as if set in motion by the wind, and not through rational impulse, like the tongues of other men : Thou art a human bell, tinkling without chime or music ! Where be the brains that should occupy thy hollow head-piece—those orts of matter that symbolize the mind ? Hast thou an eik or pertinent thereof ? Wits, like thee, should be whipped for fools.

*Swivel.* Better than being hanged for knaves,

Bill—but here come Leister and Otter. Arouse thee, Tim, and let us give noble greeting to these night-birds. I engage to swallow the whole host of their spoils, were it even ten finger-loads.

*Enter* OTTER *and* LEISTER.

*May.* Thou wilt have a dainty supper, Doctor. A dead dog! by the eye of the Cyclops!

*Leister.* O wise Bill! most sapient May-fly!

*May.* Is it not a cur, masters?

*Swivel.* Bah! Bill, art thou a hedgehog? 'tis an otter, man! The Tritons have had sport—rare sport. Egad! boys, ye are in the eyeball of Fortune; she is your mistress. Fish too, and—oh! Gaff, pull the blanket from thy temples, and have a peep at this trout! Saw you, Hackle, ever such a fly-sucker?—he is the Ammon among those other fishes, and seems as if he had sailed down Niagara, or was lessoned into prodigiousness among the waters of the Mississippi! I love the sight of him. 'Tis a heart-stirrer, and causes jealousy. I am in humour to massacre ye both, be-cause of your nocturnal achievements.—More whisky, Meg! It becomes us to drown our vexation, and you, mighty twain, to demolish before birth the effects of the night air. This brute must be stuffed and incased; —'twill form a befitting ornament to the walls of our Club-hall, and will match magnificently with our gorgeous specimen of the Loch-Awe trout, weigh-ing two stone, and altogether without a parallel in the united kingdoms of Great Britain and Ireland. But fill your tumblers—and ho! Meg, cook this fellow of a fish in a style we love, and fetch him in smoking, like a Dutchman, and girdled with viands—victuals, I mean—meats, rural and urban, of all kinds and flavours, to suit all palates, likings, and opinions. You have knocked the dormouse out of Gaff's pate, and pricked up our jaded selves once more. Skulk not, Bill; and thou, Hackle, top off thy freezing dregs, and fill anew to our worthy and scientific brothers of the angle—Tom Otter and Jack Leister! Hurra!

*Otter.* I would, Doctor, thou wert a salmon, with one of my black barbs run through the tough gristles of thy tongue. The capers of the kangaroo were not so nimble as thine would be. How thou would'st bound from the surface, and dart indignant through the water—a run of forty fathoms!—nothing less could I allow thee in a broad river like the Tweed.

*Gaff.* Let me tell thee, Tom, thou would'st find him ill to manage with seven such lengths of line. No common fish 'twould be which had the Doctor's mettle to assist it, leaving his cunning entirely out of the question. He would shake the best rod to shivers, and take the sinew out of your ablest horse-hair, almost ere your eye caught the sparkle of his broad flank, or the jut of his dorsal fin.

*Swivel.* Ay! ay! Tim, thou art right. Make a salmon of me, Master Otter! Show thyself a

Christian in thy wishes. Of a verity, would it rejoice thee to have me under thy beak, my jaw torn up with thy torture-iron—my nerves straightened, and hot with agony—my frame striving against exhaustion, and yet weaker becoming, and weaker, until the power and the spirit within it were both vanquished, and it floated into thy very grasp, only to receive its cruel death-stroke at those unsparing hands. Oh! wretch pitiless and unfeeling, insensate as marble, cold as lead!

*Otter.* A truce, worthy Doctor, a truce! Thou art bitter in thy usage of words, like a certain parson I know of, who wars, eloquently by mouth, and abuses his hearers, right and left, without check or reason. Give us a stave, Hackle, and help to restore the Doctor's good humour.

[HACKLE *sings.*]

### Bless with me the spring-tide bland.

I.

Bless with me the spring-tide bland,
   All ye anglers of the valley!
Wave aloof the slender wand,
   And around the oak-tree rally.

II.

Bless the birds, that all along
   Send us such a cheerful greeting;
To those measures of kind song
   Joyously our hearts are beating.

### III.

Fleeted now the winter snow
   From the forehead of the mountains,
And the mild sweet waters flow
   Freshly through their several fountains.

### IV.

In the secret of the sod,
   Moss and primrose lie together ;
But the wild bee shoots abroad,
   Fonder of the April heather.

### V.

Fresh and free the breezes blow,
   And the amber stream runs gaily,
Forth, and warble as ye go,
   All ye anglers of the valley !

*May.* Finely touched off, Harry. I envy thine ear and throat; they are replete with melody beyond all compare. What swells, cadences, and quavers ! Such a sea of music as thou hast within thee !

*Swivel.* Take the velvet off that tongue of thine, Master May-fly, and give us a peep of the pike's tooth. Art thou a judge in music, Bill ? 'Tis strange, of a verity—thou, May-fly, who hast neither wit nor reason, head nor heart, the voice of a dormouse, nor the ear of a landrail !—A judge in music ! Oh ! 'tis of dolorous ditties, such as bedesmen chant, of nasal drones and tooth-sawing discords, of rookery airs and toad symphonies—

caws, croaks, mews, brays and caterwaulings; —
but not of music, Bill—not of those charmed intri-
cacies of sound—those tones that soothe, and sometimes agonize — those avulsions from angel voices,
flung in among the fractured tongues at Babel's
tower;—not of these, Bill?

*May.* Mayhap of these, Doctor, I can discourse
to thee on the soul of the matter; but it is heavy
and hackneyed to talk of crotchets and semibreves,
as do your catgut men and the small school-girls of
the day. There is no cunning in the modern science
of music, more than in our modern poetry. It hath
lost its Memnonian magic;—'tis fallen and tricked
out with harlotry. What was chaste, energetic, and
solemn, has become tainted, feeble, redundant, and
grotesque. It runs not in its natural channel, but
is cooped up within angular sluice-beds, and marred
by the introduction of ill-judged embellishments.
'Tis music only to the depraved ear and the unfeeling heart. What are the songs of Italy, sung as
they are by the donnas of the scenic board, but a
replication of squalls and quavers, infinitely more
annoying than the gibberish of crones and the
yelling of jackals?

*Swivel.* Good, Bill; thou art right, though har-
pies thrust a bodkin through thy tongue. I am in
humour to love thee for this heterodoxy of thine.
'Tis sheer diablerie our modern music—diablerie
and madness. Fiddlers, pianists, flutists, harpers,

6

guitarists, organists, bellmen, and bagpipers—all are mad; and so, too, are your glee-singers and stage vocalists—your choristers and anthem-boys—your lion-throated men and rat-throated females. They deem the lungs to be the throne of the intellect, and reduce humanity to a level with cage-birds!

*Leister.* Hold, infatuated barbarian, despiser of the usages of social life! Thou hast an ear of iron and a heart of the same metal. O that I could wring thee as a sponge, or melt thee like lead at the forge! What! have the tears never issued from under those eyebrows when a dulcet melody stole into thy presence—a gush of sad, kind sounds, like the shaking of flowers or the blending of summer rainbows? Have thy thoughts never been drawn from their dull, ordinary channels, by the notes of a sweet air awakened, whether on minstrel's instrument, or flowing through the lips of some loved enchantress? What! do not the martial and naval anthems of Old England arouse the patriotic spirit within thee?—or art thou charmed never, nor yet subdued by the likenesses of joy, truth, and sorrow, embodied in our national harmonies? Art thou deaf as the adder, Doctor, and perverse as the he-bear?

*Swivel.* Go on, go on, I pray thee—nay, go on, go on, Jack—do not draw up so hastily! 'Tis a prime gallop thou art at. Scarcely can I eye thee, but thou art past my post, Master Leister, and con-

tendest with thyself alone. Spake I against thy dictum,
Jack? Not in any wise. I decried no measure of
that natural and soul-stirring music thou art propping
so vigorously. 'Tis the core of what I venerate, and
shame be to the man who injures or assails it! No,
Jack, 'twas to the modern innovations I directed my
enmity—to the mystical machines which fabricate our
popular combinations of notes and quavers—to the
German and Italian natures which are grafted upon our
orchestras, and have drunk up the sap and spirit of
what is nationally ours. The taste is low—fallen,
indeed—which prefers to the artless simplicity of
olden music the corrupt and insipid substitutes so infa-
tuatedly cherished by the amateurs of the day. But
thy song, Jack—thy stave—and, mind thee, no extra
flourishes or off-shows.

[LEISTER *sings.*]

### The Anglers' Trysting-tree.

I.

Sing, sweet thrushes, forth and sing !
  Meet the morn upon the lea ;
Are the emeralds of spring
  On the anglers' trysting-tree ?
Tell, sweet thrushes, tell to me,
Are·there buds on our willow tree ?—
  Buds and birds on the trysting-tree ?

### II.

Sing, sweet thrushes, forth and sing !
  Have you met the honey-bee,
Circling upon rapid wing
  Round the anglers' trysting-tree ?
Up, sweet thrushes, up and see ;
Are there bees at our willow tree ?—
  Birds and bees at the trysting-tree ?

### III.

Sing, sweet thrushes, forth and sing !
  Are the fountains gushing free ?
Is the south wind wandering
  Thro' the anglers' trysting-tree ?
Up, sweet thrushes, tell to me,
Is the wind at our willow tree ?—
  Wind or calm at the trysting-tree ?

### IV.

Sing, sweet thrushes, up and sing !
  Wile us, with a merry glee,
To the flowery haunts of spring—
  To the anglers' trysting-tree !
Tell, sweet thrushes, tell to me,
Are there flowers 'neath our willow tree ?—
  Spring and flowers at the trysting-tree ?

*Otter.* 'Tis a pity we have so meagre a fund of good angling songs. Most of our modern poets are, or have been, brethren of the streams; and yet who among them has ventured to weave us a melody in honour of his favourite craft ? Scott, Burns, Wilson, Wordsworth, and the Ettrick Shep-

herd, all of them well and devotedly loved our pastime. It matters nothing to us! They have left of
their attachment no relic in immortal rhymes. We
marvel, but do not upbraid them. They have written
on loftier themes, and sought therefore a loftier meed
of honour than the discourse of a few wandering
anglers could possibly confer.

*Hackle.* You say truly. Man was their study—
man, under the dominion of nature and his own fellow-
creatures—man, with his heart, and its world of con-
flicting passions—man that drops from the womb into
the cradle, and, springing from thence, gathers, with
the winds, power and knowledge, until the star of
independence settles upon his forehead, and he shivers
with one strong impulse all derogatory bonds, showing
himself what he is, a son of his Maker, in frame and
intellect equal to any king. 'Tis a theme exhaustless
and illimitable, as it is to reckon and compute the
surges of the sea; they change in number, feature,
body and altitude, in sound and in transparency; so
do men. The matter is not worn out, as some small
critics happen to imagine, who, to appear sagacious,
assume a knowledge of human nature, even the tithe
of whose workings is to them an incomprehensible
hieroglyph. Have they the key of a single heart,
among the plotting, careworn, joyous, jealous, and
distressful numbers, that throbs along the highway
of life? Can they lay bare the actuating motives
for a solitary deed, performed by any being? They

may infer, but they cannot divulge: inferences are not truth——

*May.* Hold, Harry, and prate within limit. Wilt thou strangle us at feast-time with thy dry logic and dusty philosophy? Is't not better, think you, to make a book on't, which the dull may read at pleasure, than force it adown our throats against all inclination? But now another song; I love thy snatches marvellously; they reach to my inner man, and stir the pith of my nature.

*Hackle.* Strike up thyself, Bill——come to light with a love-lilt.

*May.* I, Master Hackle!——warble forsooth! Heard you Doctor Swiveltop opining concerning me?

*Swivel.* Spilt words, Bill; we revoke them with good-will. Truly, May-fly, thou art the ablest of able performers, albeit, like other great men, sprinkled with conceit of thyself. Nay, man, I miscalled thee not, save with the intent of reducing thy vanity. 'Tis a monster thou should'st put in irons, else the fingers of it will tighten around thy throat with the clutch of a hyena. But thou *canst* sing, Bill——thou *canst* play upon thy windpipe, and knowest it to boot. Be not backward, or sham modesty, like a school-girl; start into metres, as the bards of Fingal did; throw out a bravura from the hollow of thy lungs, or be plaintive and exceeding tender, as "a love-sick pigeon!"

*May.* You distress me, Doctor, beyond measure.

Vanity ! modesty ! eh !—what else ? But have my stave, boys, and welcome ! [*Sings.*]

### The Sea-trout gray.

#### I.

The sea-trout gray
Are now at play,
   The salmon is up—hurra ! hurra !
For the streamlets brown
Are dancing down ;
   So quicken the cup—hurra ! hurra !

#### II.

The cloud-cap still
Is on the hill,
   And the showers fall fast—hurra ! hurra !
But the sun and breeze
Will scatter these ;
   So drink while they last—hurra ! hurra !

#### III.

We'll start by dawn,
O'er lea and lawn,
   Through thicket and thorn—hurra ! hurra !
On merriest limb,
With rods in trim ;
   Come, drink a sweet morn—hurra ! hurra !

*All.* Hurra ! hurra !

*May.* And now, masters, that ye have got it, what think ye of it ?

*Hackle.* O, 'tis the pride of melodies, and might win its way before caliphs!

*Leister.* 'Tis witching as a star-song.

*Gaff.* 'Tis jeopardy for a damsel to list to't.

*Otter.* Let us build a shrine.

*Swivel.* Ay, Otter, you have it; we will erect a column—no, a mosque, a temple, a pyramid—ay, a pyramid, with vaulty labyrinths and Sphinx-dens, wherein to embody—what? thee, Bill? Nay, but thy song personified in shape of a——but here enters supper. It dips the eye of an ogre into one's forehead to peep at such a stalwart fish. O, Leister! 'twas a noble catch, worthy a king's toil. I'd rather the turning of that broad flank than the control of an armed legion on such a field as glorious Waterloo —even so.

*Leister.* Let us devour, Doctor, thanking heaven. I have two plump flappers before me, bred among bulrushes—dainty birds I warrant them.

*May.* They tickle the lamina of my palate. A breast-cut and the left thigh-bone, if you please.

*Leister.* The left, Bill!—Ere long there will be nothing left at this rate.

*May.* 'Tis plain, thou art right, Jack; forget not to administer an onion.

*Leister.* I shall seize on thee otherwise, Bill, an' thou art longer clamorous. How now, Doctor, no duck?

*Swivel.* Keep a reserve, old boy. My first attack is on the fish—my second on these choice-looking morsels of mutton—then, for a semi-flapper from thee—and I shall crown all by quarrying into the heart of yonder ewe-milk kebbock.

*Hackle.* This is supping with a vengeance!

*Swivel.* Say you, Harry? Any pigeons-eggs on the table for our friend Hackle? He hasn't the appetite of a tom-tit. These arms of thine want brawn, Harry; and these legs—ha! ha! Didst thou ever behold a well-shaped, unhosed, and finely-rounded limb without blushing at the poor, scraggy, and unfortunate shanks on which thou thyself trudgest? 'Tis a pity, man, the art of flesh-gathering is so rare with thee. See Tom Otter, there, and Tim Gaff—ay, and the rest of us—we have more than skin and bones—we are not dry, rattling bags, like our great-grandmothers; and why? 'tis past nature we should be otherwise; see how we eat!

*Hackle.* Stuff, cram, gorge!

*May.* Not so, Master Hackle; I for one am esteemed singularly abstemious. I have no whirl-pool within me, like these honest gentlemen. I don't discuss a mutton at a meal, nor shake a firlot of eggs down my throat at breakfast, as some of *them* do. Am *I* stuffed, crammed, and gorged?

*Hackle.* Gluttonous beyond measure, Bill.

*May.* Listen, O ye shades of doughty warriors! to whom a sirloin of stout beef was as a matter of moonshine—ye who could tuck under your noble

ribs what a modern can scarce stride across, who
swallowed bacons entire, and measured your brose
with a cauldron!—listen and wonder! O the de-
generacy of the age! the spare-thrift and rigid
self-denial of us manikins! How are we shrunk
and become sickly, having weak lives and sad di-
gestions? What think ye of Harry Hackle, the
scarecrow?—this thin, pill-purged, frog-kneed an-
atomy!

*Otter.* Eat, Bill, eat; you make no supper, man.
Hackle will hurl his fork betwixt your jaws, unless
you employ them to better purpose.

*Hackle.* Ay will I, Master May-fly.

*May.* Is he wrathful, Tom? Hath he the canine
tooth? Can he bite?

*Otter.* Do not tempt him, Bill; lean sharks are
least to be trusted. But what is this?—a letter,
Meg.

*Enter* MEG *with a letter.*

" To the worthy and able Anglers assembled at
—— Inn." This is something facetious.

*Leister.* A beggar's petition haply.

*Otter.* Nay, Jack; the paper is of honest size
and quality, clean withal, is well waxed, and neatly
impressed.

" GENTLEMEN,

        " Understanding that you intend to reside a few
days in this neighbourhood for the purpose of amusement,

and that you reckon among you more than one angler
of celebrity, we, the undersigned, being similarly situated,
are anxious that, as the river is broad, convenient, and in good
condition, a trial of skill should take place betwixt an equal
number of your party and two of ourselves—say to-morrow,
or any other day of this week which you may find suitable.
The fly only to be used, and the contest to commence and
terminate at fixed hours, and under such restrictions as may
be agreed upon before starting ;—the party losing to forfeit a
dinner. Should this proposal meet with your approbation,
you will not refuse us the honour of breakfasting with us to-
morrow, at half-past seven, and settling the preliminaries.

" We remain, although strangers, brethren of the craft,
and your very obedient humble servants,

" RICHARD HERON-BILL.
MARK WANDLE-WEIR.
ANTHONY SMOULTER-JAWS.

*All.* Agreed, agreed.

*Swivel.* So say we, masters : but who are these
Goliaths of Gath that come out against us ?

*Hackle.* It matters not ; they offer fair, and will
fight honestly.

*May.* 'Tis a civil challenge they send us. To
refuse is to kill our own good repute. Let us re-
spond—and arm.

*Swivel.* What ! thou, Bill ! thou engage to kill a
crocodile, who art slow to master a minnow ! Nay,
most valiant May-fly, aback, and learn modesty !
It behoves our heroes of to-night to represent us,

and not thee. Stand forth, Jack Leister and Tom Otter, stand forth! Ye are our men of pride, and these bones bear witness to you! Yon grim, huge head, gapes monarchically from the dish, where it lies and proclaims your merits. And you, gentlemen, what say you?

*All.* Leister and Otter for ever!

*Leister.* You greatly honour our poor abilities, Doctor;—but be it so. How, Tom, are you disposed? Shall we obey the commonwealth?

*Otter.* I object not, aided by so powerful an ally; yet, or I am mistaken, these rival brethren of the craft, who so self-confidently challenge us, are neither raw nor undisciplined. I know one of them already by repute—Wandle-weir, an Englishman, I believe, and one well versed in all the mysteries of the art. However, 'tis more endurable to be vanquished by men of skill, than have a fair name taken from us through vulgar and dishonest craft, such as is practised against strangers by the dons of a small watering-place on Tweedside. But we must send a reply.

*Swivel.* Be thou our secretary, Harry, and so dictate:

" GENTLEMEN,

"We gave ready welcome to your note of challenge, and have selected two out of our body, willing to compete with you on the proposed terms. We suggest moreover, that the contest shall take place to-morrow, and accordingly shall avail ourselves of your polite invitation to breakfast at half-past seven exactly, when umpires shall be chosen, hours determined, and other preliminaries settled.

> " We are, gentlemen, your obedient humble servants,
> and brother anglers,

| | |
|---|---|
| " J. LEISTER. | H. HACKLE. |
| T. OTTER. | T. GAFF. |
| N. SWIVELTOP. | W. MAY-FLY." |

*Gaff*. Excellent, Doctor! Address to "The Honourable Fraternity of Anglers now residing at —— Inn."

*Swivel*. Even so; and now let us append the crest of our club—a salmo rampant—with the motto. [*Enter Meg.*] Ho! Meg—who waits?

*Meg*. A boy, sir.

*Swivel*. Let him run like a twinkling, and deliver this, he knows where. [*Exit Meg.*] We must be up with the larks. Is your tackle in readiness, Jack? and yours, Tom? Ay! ay! always ready. Read us the barometer, Harry.

*Hackle*. Inclined to rise, Doctor.

*Swivel*. 'Tis all the better. The water is still in good trim—a degree too small, but more room for display of science. And now, as it is not very late, let us draw out a code of river-regulations for the protection and advantage of the competitors. We can submit them for approval before the contest commences, to those gentlemen who have thrown down the gauntlet; and I have no doubt they will cordially acquiesce in the arrangements we propose making. But clear the table, Meg, and bring glasses; we can do nothing without the jug social; our wits won't work without it.

[During the dictation of these by the worthy Doctor, assisted by Jack Leister and Tom Otter, Gaff slyly slunk away to bed, and Bill May-fly stood at the shutters, amusing himself with an apostrophe to the moon, part of which is preserved in the MS. scroll of regulations drawn out in the neat and diminutive hand of Harry Hackle, Esq., who obviously took advantage of certain pauses in the Doctor's composition to preserve this singular record.]

*May.* Ha! my maiden moon, astart to-night! Have the sun-vampires stolen the blood from thee? Thou art ever blenched in the forehead, and solemn of countenance. Hast no saffron to heighten thy complexion?—Lack-a-day! why dost thou rob me of my laughs and frolics? Thy melancholy is catching. Ah! my fair mistress thou hast none of the merry twinkling these stars have—nothing humorous about thee. Why come hither? Art thou on an embassage to tearful lovers? Oh! thou'rt a false witch, and pryest into our crimes and calamities. Aback! aback! there is nothing for thy search beyond these shutters—no sorrows here madam; and yet, not good-night—'twould be an early parting to bid good-night so soon, and to one so lovely. Was't thus in the beginning—and did father Adam gaze on thee ? Did Egyptian Sesostris, and he of Macedon, and Hannibal, and the Caesars, and Tamerlane, and Mahomet ? Did Hesiod, Homer, and Sappho ? Did Shakspeare and Milton ?—Come ! thou'rt familiar with all these, and hast their histories at heart. Nigh six millenniums must have unfolded wonders ! How many battlefields hast thou ridden across ! how many plague-struck realms, void of joy ! Oh ! ours are but dull, tame times to thee, when empires are at peace. 'Tis no spectacle, this commercial theatre, like the war-field. Come, ope thy lips ! Why so chary of thy knowledge ? Say, what thou seest now ?—what of navies in the broad blue sea ?—what of slumbering cities and tented armies ?—what of forests, wolf-infested ?—of rueful wastes, stupendous mountains, and mighty rivers ? Is thine eye on the pyramids, and thy soul back among the Pharaohs ? Art thou mingling thine with the cold silvers of their north, or dost thou lace the waves, washing up the corals to the very roots of broad-leaved palms, around an Indian isle ?

[The MS. soliloquy assumes at this point such a fragmentary appearance that we are induced to omit a considerable portion of what remains. The following appears to be its conclusion.]

What dost thou with a cloud ? O treachery ! the ship is on a rock !—Ha ! forth again, to show his

grave to many a breathing mariner?—Good-night,
thou hag of mischief! What are horrors to thee,
before whom stalk our feud and pestilence—our out-
rage and calamity? Lift not thou the angler's curtain;
'tis no blessing to have thy prostituted light shed on
his slumbering forehead. Away! he provokes thee
not; get thee homage from the bandit and jackal.
Good-night—good-night!

[After this extraordinary effusion, Mr. May-fly thought
proper to follow the example of Tim Gaff, leaving the
remainder of our worthy anglers still busily engaged
in framing and counter-framing such enactments as
were necessary, they severally opined, to preserve the
balance of the competition. The result of their labours,
was as follows. It is unnecessary to add, that on sub-
mitting the regulations next morning to the contending party, they received a cordial and unanimous approval, and a vote of thanks was immediately tendered
to the industrious projectors.]

### LAWS OF COMPETITION,

AS SUBMITTED DURING BREAKFAST ON THE FOLLOWING MORN-
ING TO THE PARTY OF ANGLERS AT H——N INN.

I. That the arrangements already settled in previous communications betwixt parties shall be held as binding.

II. That umpires shall be appointed, one by each party, to
overlook the observance of regulations by the competitors, and
decide the contest.

III. That no individual shall be allowed to join in the competition, who is not at the starting-post precisely at nine o'clock, A.M.; but the absence of such individual shall not exclude the contest, should the remaining competitor, in his reduced position, think proper to commence it. The non-appearance of an entire party shall of course occasion the forfeiture of the stake.

IV. That the competitors shall again appear at the starting-post at five o'clock, P.M., when the match shall be held terminated, and the umpires called upon to decide.

V. That the place of contest shall be confined to the river itself, all tributaries excluded.

> A slight objection was raised on the part of Mr. Wandle-weir to this enactment; but as he avoided carrying it to any length, it was generally concluded that he was secretly not displeased at its introduction.

VI. That, upon starting, the two contending parties shall proceed in different directions, as shall be decided by lot; one up and the other down the river, and to such a distance, that before commencing to angle, there shall be at least a full English mile of water betwixt them.

VII. That each party shall include the umpire chosen by its opponents—who, however, shall not be entitled to angle, or to interrupt, in any way, the progress of the contest.

> Both of these regulations were canvassed by Mr. Wandle-weir, who proposed, that the competitors should be set off, one against the other, on opposite banks of the river. He agreed, however, to the division into two

7

parties, although he questioned the expediency of hamper-
ing them with the presence of umpires. It was argued
on the side of the club, that to approximate the competitors to each other in the manner proposed, might be apt
to occasion too great a spirit of rivalry betwixt them, and
have the effect of marring those feelings of ultimate concord which it was desirable to establish. Again, the club
could with difficulty understand how the presence of
umpires could be felt as a restraint. If it were so, the
restraint was a mutual one. In their opinion, however,
it was a manifest relief ; the duties of the umpires being
to preserve betwixt the parties a strict line of disunion,
and to announce to those competing the pre-occupation by
stranger anglers of such pools as lay in advance. These
explanations were admitted by Mr. Wandle-weir to be
perfectly satisfactory, and he accordingly withdrew his
amendment.

VIII. That the artificial fly alone shall be angled with, and
no cross-lines adopted.

IX. That no competitor shall be allowed an assistant.

X. That the fish captured shall be estimated by weight, and
not by number.

XI. That should one of the competitors happen to produce a
grilse or salmon (of which there are a few at present in the
water), the capture of such fish being with the trouting-fly a
matter of chance more than of skill, it shall not be reckoned,
however large, to exceed the weight of three pounds.

To this regulation the most cordial assent was given by
Mr. Wandle-weir and the other gentlemen present ; and
after discussing a few minor preliminaries, among
which the dinner was taken into ample consideration,
the two parties started, precisely as the clock struck
nine, from the small parlour in H——n Inn. Dr.

Swiveltop, unanimously elected umpire on the side of the club, accompanied Messrs. Wandle-weir and Heron-bill up the river ; while Smoulter-jaws, the other arbiter of the contest, along with Jack Leister and Tom Otter, proceeded in the contrary direction. Hackle, May-fly, and Tim Gaff, set off towards a neighbouring loch to dabble for perch and set pike-lines.

# CHAPTER V.

## INTERIOR OF A POOL ON THE RIVER.

*Enter two* TROUT.

*1st Trout.* 'Tis getting on in the summer, comrade; we shall have a hatch of stone-flies ere long, and fill our bellies quietly, without risk of being tongue-grappled by a treacherous torture-iron, in shape of a fat insect. Ay! we shall have to pick and choose upon, and can look before we leap.

*2d Trout.* This caution, neighbour, won't work always. Should I, for instance, take to conjecturing about a fine morsel I see floating towards me, up pops a hungry-headed kelt or some such grim glutton, and away it vanishes. Speculation would make us as lean as eels; so better trust to chance than take to suspicion. However, as you say, this weather will give us abundance—see, there are swallows abroad. I lately overheard Clang-chops, the old pike, say to fat uncle Baunch, after both had taken their suppers, and one might venture near them with impunity, that he had not infrequently made a spring after one of these birds, but found their feathers hard of digestion. By-the-bye, I have not observed our worthy uncle on the feed this morning. Think you he is unwell?

*1st Trout.* No wonder, he over-eats himself. I have no compassion for the glutton, and, should he pop off, will immediately take possession of his castle, being next of kin, and older than yourself by four seasons. But come, let us have a peep at him, and inquire after his health. How is this?—he is not here; 'tis strange indeed! Is't possible he has changed his residence? But no, everything so comfortable;— at his time of life, too, quite impossible! But what news, Master White-fin?

*Enter another* TROUT.

*3d Trout.* News! why is't not news enough, that King Baunch is no more?

*1st Trout.* My fat uncle no more!

*3d Trout.* Alas! indeed—he was captured by one of the land-craft no later than yester-eve.

*1st Trout.* What! out-witted too! my clever, close, sapient uncle, out-witted with a feather! 'Tis a lesson, faith, and a good one. I shan't eye food for a fort-night, no, nor venture from home neither;—and now that I think on't, I may as well reside here, since the old boy's gone. 'Tis a quiet, retired place, and no bustle about it to tempt me abroad. But ho! 'ware pike, comrades! here comes old Clang-chops to look after his neighbour.

*2d Trout.* The wily ruffian! I shall round and have a sly bite at his tail. He did the same office to me some months ago; but he was nimbler on the tack then than he is at present. I wish some of the land-craft had taken him instead of uncle Baunch, who, praise to his memory! never devoured above one of his own progeny at a meal. This fellow thinks nothing of whipping up half a score of us!

*Exeunt* Trout.

*Enter* Pike.

*Pike.* Hollo!—King Baunch, up, thou oily knave! and account to me for the rumpus thou madest after sunset yesterday. One would have fancied that Sir Otter had a hold of thy spine-bone! Now that I think on't, thou owest me still for protection against the robber nine dainty par and half a gross of minnows— ay, and for last night's slumber too; besides, not a bite came my way, owing to these capers of thine. Your majesty must tell down ere long, or I shall hoist my war-fin, and show the bloody tooth. But what, King Baunch! art afraid to come out of thy castle? Might I not blockade and starve thee in't? Show face, like an honest fellow, and fear nothing. Answer, friend— art deaf? I roar enough, don't I? What is the matter,

King Baunch? Ha! not at home?—'tis strange, and after breakfast too—against his custom.

*Enter* TROUT, *and retires, after snapping at the* PIKE'S *tail.*

My tail! this is audacity! a blackguard eel, no doubt—loathsome pest! There's no checking the freedoms these wretches use with our anointed persons —and then they screw themselves under ground ere we can get a peep at them. But this bite is a confounded sharp one, and no eel's neither, but a traitor trout's. King Baunch's mayhap; the sagacious knave! he shall suffer for it. Methinks, however, I should have had a glimpse of his unwieldy flanks, wheeling round, as I did, so readily. Revenge is my motto, and away I set to deal heavy havoc for this act of aggression! The starry-sides, I warrant them, will soon come to terms.

*Exit* PIKE.

*Re-enter three* TROUT.

*1st Trout.* You managed old Clang-chops neatly! He is in a fearful fury, and swears destruction to our whole tribe, dashing this way and that, whisking his tail and grinding his teeth.

*2d Trout.* He is as blind as a worm, and will run himself ashore ere long. Poor King Baunch was accustomed to catch half his dinner for him, and no small matter it was. He hasn't a slice of the wits of our late sovereign——and with a resolute master, I have no doubt we could force him to abandon the pool.

*3d Trout.* 'Twould be a praiseworthy action.

*2d Trout.* Not so, Master White-fin. Who is our safe-guard against Sir Otter?

*3d Trout.* Why! 'tis rumoured he is dead also.

*2d Trout.* Strange rumours these, if true.

*3d Trout.* Moreover, 'tis whispered the land-craft are abroad.

*1st Trout.* Ay! plain enough, Master White-fin. They have a hand in these butcheries, no doubt. But see what a sweet morsel above thee——a prime fly. Thou'rt lean in the shoulders, and hast need of food; I yield it.

*3d* TROUT *rises, and finds himself fixed.*

*3d Trout.* Oh! oh!—help! help!

*1st Trout.* What! trapped? have they a hold of thee, loon? Good-bye, good-bye; come away, comrade.

*2d Trout.* He's past rescue, methinks. Adieu, Master White-fin.

*Exeunt* 1st *and* 2d TROUT.

*3d Trout.* Oh! ungrateful traitors, will nothing save me? Three times have I leapt upwards, twice have I sounded the channel, and once have I made for my den across the stream. I must e'en come ashore now. Alack-a-day!

*3d* TROUT *is dragged off.*

This very fictitious chapter is evidently the joint composition of Harry Hackle and Bill May-fly, who appear to have written it on the day of the competition, and while watching, in company with Tim Gaff, an array of pike trimmers floating along the reedy margins of Loch ————. Their success was limited, but they professed to have derived considerable amusement from the number of nibbles they encountered, and which Tom Otter thought fit, greatly to their wrath and vexation, to attribute to one small-headed, but particularly hungry eel.

# CHAPTER VI.

## WANDLE-WEIR AND HERON-BILL.

*Enter* MARK WANDLE-WEIR *and* RICHARD HERON-BILL,
*on opposite sides of the river.*

*Wandle.* Absolutely, Dick, I have a mind to hang myself upon this very tree. No less than three casts of choice flies have I anchored already among its boughs, and all while attempting to strike one dull-headed trout, who persists in rising tail foremost, or something very like it. Yet I have no wish to leave the booby without a taste of the cold steel. Were you able to manage from that side of the water, a fly-trailer is certain to start him; he lies to the right of yonder stone, and will steady your basket beautifully, weighing upwards of a pound. Throw higher up and softly; ay, he broke the surface. You draw your flies too rapidly.

*Heron.* Not a bit, he is tired of us. But how get you on, Wandle-weir? 'Tis slow work with me as yet;—nothing save a few par and one satanic-looking creature I took out of the last stream, having a large black head and inky breast. 'Twill be made a question whether it belong to the trout species or not. The umpire has his doubts.

*Wandle.* I have the lead of you, but not greatly. However, 'tis only eleven, and the fish are just commencing their forenoon feed. An hour or two will make us better contented. Try the March-brown. 'Tis a late insect on this water compared with what it is in England. A light hare's-ear body is also commendable.

*Heron.* My upper dropper is a small Limerick, with blue jay feather, yellow hackle and silver twist.

*Wandle.* Ridiculous! off with it, as you value your own repute. A Scotchman in this quarter would laugh at you, and ask how many " puddocks " you had bagged. The fal-de-rols hereabouts will achieve nothing; reserve them for August, and our intended trip to the north-west; they may answer well with the sea-trout and salmon.

*Heron.* Would you advise a brown palmer fly?

*Wandle.* By all means, but let it be small—one degree bigger than a midge.

*Heron.* I have what will suit exactly.—You hold a good trout, or I mistake.

*Wandle.* He seems a fair fish, and obstinate too;

however, walk into my pannier, friend. — Hollo
Dick !

*Heron.* Another !

*Wandle.* A brace, I believe ;—there is one at my
trail-fly also, but neither of them are large.   You see
they begin to do us homage.

*Heron.* So I observe.   Look what a world of them
are agog in yonder stream !—why, every inch of water
is alive ; let us down to it, and give no quarter.

*Wandle.* Remain where you are, Dick, if you are
wise.   Take my word for it you'll not capture a single
fin.   'Tis the same on this very pool.   See, how the
March-browns are descending !—Our feathers can do
nothing among such tempters.

*Heron.* Sad enough ! my mouth waters at the sight
of these great fellows popping up every mortal second,
and no way to run our hooks athwart them.   I have
one in jeopardy, however ; he is but tenderly fastened,
and I must wile him in among the levels.


*Enter* SWIVELTOP.


*Swivel.* You will teach our club humility, gentlemen.   Of a truth they may abandon the contest ; but
I fear I disturb you, Mr. Heron-bill.

*Heron.* Not so, Doctor ; I angle all the better now
that you are with me ; believe me you are no mar-
sport, and aid wonderfully in keeping up my courage—

*Swivel.* Which I had as lief see extinguished.

Nay, if my company prop thee, 'tis well. I love to look on an able angler. It kills all jealousy, and, to tell the truth, 'tis with me a matter of indifference *which* turns out to be the winning party, provided each individual so performs as to win the respect of his rivals.

*Heron.* I agree with you entirely, and shall not take a defeat to heart so deeply as my friend Wandle-weir; however, fight I shall, were my bones to crack.

*Swivel.* A wise resolution. You pricked a pretty fish just now.

*Heron.* Ay, but he is gone. I hit him on his reflective organ; he will abjure flies during this forenoon at least. Wandle-weir, I perceive, has something weighty at his lines, and—ha! ha!—a dead sheep—what a trophy! Into your pannier with it, Mark, should you land him!

*Wandle.* 'Tis an excellent Cheviot, Dick, and in glorious order—very savoury, I assure you; but, alas! I must bid good-bye to it, for my flies are clear, and a tiny par, moreover, dangling at the trailer. I trust, Doctor, you compassionate our miseries.

*Swivel.* Not a whit—how should I, when I behold your good fortune? nay, nay, Mr. Wandle-weir, thou art loading thy shoulders in style. Show them some charity, an' thou lovest them.

*Wandle.* They merit little; my pannier has only three brace of honest-sized fish in't, none of which weigh above thirteen ounces; as for the others, you would positively laugh to see them. But, by the three Graces! there is a raree-show, a girl of sweet nineteen crossing the ford. Look, Dick!—such a symmetry of limb and ancle—what a vision! 'tis worth the gold of a sculptor. Ha! she observes us, and now drops her robes, but not altogether. She is knee-deep, and evidently embarrassed. There is no help for it; so on she goes, blushing and laughing by turns. This is genuine modesty in distress, Dick!—a prude so situated would get angry—a flirt stumble into a hole, as if by accident, but for no other purpose than exciting sympathy, bringing assistance, and giving a certain celestial impulse to her drapery.

*Heron.* I am glad the poor thing has got over safely, without any such awkward mischance as you allude to. 'Twas a small measure of forbearance we granted her, watching her attitudes so narrowly. She is in full retreat to yon farm-house—and God bless her!

So endeth this chapter, and wisely. The remarks of anglers, when deeply engaged in the sport, are, besides being limited, somewhat monotonous; and for this reason, we presume, the club has given us no insight into the operations of the other contending party, further than a bare statement of the amount of fish produced by each competitor at the close of the contest. It stood as follows:—

| | | | LARGEST TROUT. | |
|---|---|---|---|---|
| Captured with the fly by Jack Leister, | LBS. | OZ. | LBS. | OZ. |
| 16th May, 18—, . . . | 37 | . 7 | 2 | . 3½ |
| By Tom Otter, ditto, . . | 31 | . 6 | 2 | . 7 |
| Sum total, | 68 | . 13 | | |
| Captured by Mark Wandle-weir, 16th | LBS. | OZ. | | |
| May, 18—, . . . | 30 | . 13 | | |
| By Richard Heron-bill, ditto, . | 21 | . 1 | | |
| Sum total, | 51 | . 14 | | |
| | 68 | . 13 | | |
| Balance in favour of the club, | 16 | . 15 | | |

(Signed)  ANTHONY SMOULTER-JAWS.
NATHAN SWIVELTOP.

Accordingly, the club competitors were by the umpires declared victorious.

Of course, some chagrin was felt by Mr. Wandle-weir upon this declaration, and testified, besides, by a challenge immediately given to Jack Leister to compete with him next morning, single-handed, and on opposite banks of the river—no wading permitted, as it seems this worthy and excellent member of our club generally adopted the heron-mode of angling, to which system was attributed the whole of his present success. Leister, without hesitation, agreed to take part in the contest, which being decided on the following afternoon, the result was immensely in Jack's favour. He ran no less than 15 lbs. ahead of his opponent, and accordingly ended all disputes about the matter. Meanwhile, the feelings of disappointment at first exhibited by Mr. Wandle-weir soon wore off, and he united with great good-will in the lengthened festivities of the evening—a record of which seems to have been originally pre-served among the club papers. Upon this we have been unable to lay our hands. It appears, however, from inquiry and recollection, that Messrs. Wandle-weir, Heron-bill, and Smoulter-jaws, were with due ceremony, and at their own request, admitted in the course of the same evening members of the club, and made entitled to its various immunities and priv-ileges.

# CHAPTER VII.

## THE NORTHERN LOCHS AND RIVERS.

### LEISTER, WANDLE-WEIR, AND HERL-BROKE.

*Leister.* You intend, Mr. Wandle-weir, I understand, to investigate our Northern Lochs and Rivers. You will find many of them excellent, especially those in the counties of Inverness, Ross, and Sutherland; which, however, are for the most part strictly watched over, and carefully preserved.

*Wandle.* Indeed, sir, I was not aware of any restriction imposed upon trout-fishers throughout this part of Britain.

*Leister.* Agreeably to the laws of our ancient realm, there are none. Trout are reckoned as *res nullius,* and the property of those that can capture them. But, sir, you must understand that our northern landholders have a law with themselves in regard to this matter, which, as no patriotic individual has

8

as yet thought it worth his while to dispute, is kept in severe practice against all who infringe upon it. In Sutherland especially you will find it in its fullest force. Belonging, it may be said, to a single proprietor, this immense territory is controlled upon a system which infringes very considerably upon Scottish privileges. Its numerous lochs and rivers, where the destruction would scarcely be noticed were an army of us scattered among them to angle for a century, all these are in a manner shut up against the craft, nor is it an easy matter to acquire access to them.

*Wandle.* And Ross-shire ?—Do these innovations upon public rights extend to it also ?

*Leister.* Partly to every shire in the north of Scotland. You perceive in our southern districts, however, we are able to keep ourselves free from such unhallowed interference on the part of the landholders, who well know that all measures taken to check anglers in the peaceful exercise of their pastime must prove abortive—provided, of course, they have established by usage a right of access to the water-edge, otherwise the tenant of the lands through which they pass has it in his power to pursue them as trespassers. In the counties I have alluded to, a mere action of trespass could scarcely be supported in any court, unless damage had actually and conjointly been effected—a thing next to impossible among moorland wastes, and along the unrestrained channels of the rapid rivers. The soil, unless planted

or cultivated, is free to all. Even some of its posses-
sors do not dispute this ; but display your angling-rod,
and you will have keepers immediately at your side,
charging you to change the scene of your operations.

*Wandle.* And were one to resist their authority,
what would be the consequences ?

*Leister.* The immediate ones would of course be
greatly against the party challenged, although I cannot persuade myself but that the proprietor, unless
holding the water and its fishings directly from the
crown, would ultimately be the loser—at least, the case
never having been pushed to any proper determination, I am urged, upon legal principles, to believe so.
Alas ! Mr. Wandle-weir, they know little who imagine
of Scotland that her hills are the dwelling-places of
the free—they dream not of the inroads of gigantic
monopolies athwart the rights and liberties of her
children—of lords of the soil expatriating their vas-
sals—usurping public and prescriptive privileges—
acting the unchallenged despot over every foot of
their petty dominions. But so it is ! An unnatural policy is in force under the outworks of the true
constitution, neither assisted nor yet opposed by
state machinery—the spirit of a system, which threat-
ens to reassume and concentrate the barbarous in-
vestitures of feudal ages. These are excrescences
upon the trunks of power, displacing every humble
hindrance to their growth, often through legal wile
and artifice, but oftener by the strong arm of might.

The aggressions of men of influence in the north are becoming every day bolder—the attitudes assumed by them more and more insolent. They distort the ear of justice, trample upon the prerogatives of the people, delete the most sacred charters, and encircle with a palisado of obnoxious enactments their ill-gotten acquisitions.

*Wandle.* This is a sad picture of things, Mr. Leister, and bids fair, Herl-broke, to knock our projected excursion on the head.

*Leister.* Nay, gentlemen, I have no such design, and would only depress a trifle your preconceived notions of Highland liberality. You may find, however, this praise-besplattered virtue better exemplified by experiencing the proofs on't. By all means trip it northwards—you will not want amusement, and, if sketchers as well as anglers, may occasionally drop in among enviable masses of scenery, choice groupings of tree, hill, and water, well worthy of your attention. Among our club papers, by-the-bye, we have several communications from different members of our fraternity regarding various waters in the districts of Scotland you intend visiting. You are welcome, should you desire it, to a perusal of these, and I have no doubt they will afford you some minute information with respect to the angling qualifications of such lochs and rivers as you are likely to fall in with during your tour.

*Wandle.* You greatly oblige us, Mr. Leister, and I, for my part, shall certainly take advantage of your offer, as also, I have no doubt, will my friend Herl-broke. What say you, Dick ?

*Herl.* Most thankfully and by all means.

The above is a fragment of conversation which took place betwixt Messrs. Leister, Wandle-weir, and Herl-broke, previous to the departure of the two latter gentlemen for the north of Scotland. As in the course of it allusion is made to certain papers communicated by members of the club, we think it proper, having obtained possession of one or more of · these, to insert them in this place, premising, that they appear to us generally, if not specifically correct. The following is an account of some of the streams and lochs belonging to Easter Ross-shire.

## LOCH ACHILTY, ROSS-SHIRE.

THERE are few lakes in Scotland so attractive as Loch Achilty. It is situated in a forest of natural birch, the more graceful of our British trees. On one side stands its own Tor, the nursery of our northern red-deer ; on the other rises Craigdarroch, a wild accumulation of rocks and masses. Both hills are plentifully wooded, and have a thick, waist-deep heather covering in many parts. Loch Achilty is a singular piece of water—singular in its make, its workings, and its produce. It has several inlets, and, strange to say, no visible outlet. The bottom is of a softish substance, full of springs, and strewn over with trunks of sunken trees that have lain there for ages. Although fed from a mossy origin by dark-coloured streams, the water of Loch Achilty is during summer pure and crystalline, unlike that of Loch Nech-Beann, or the Lake of the White-Horse, above Towie, out of which, and through a smaller tarn, its principal feeder comes. In this uppermost loch are found fine-sized red-trout, which dash eagerly at the fly towards gloaming, but at other times are shy or asleep, for they rise infrequently and with more circumspection; yet one may occasionally capture a dozen or two of them by nice management, and this number will fill a common-sized creel to the very brim. There is a heronry on a small island within this mountain reservoir, which is well worthy of observation.

The middle sheet of water, Loch-an-Drame, lying down in a fairy-haunted hollow, teems with small, lively fish. In Loch Achilty itself, the trout, though by no means large, are yet well-sized, and singularly strong. When hooked, they make directly for the bottom, and cause an uncommon vibratory sensation along the line. They are not remarkably thick-shaped, but the head is small, and the flesh red and well-flavoured.

The most curious production of Loch Achilty is its char. This beautiful fish is indeed discovered in a number of our Scottish lakes, but nowhere have we found it so eager in its approaches towards the fly as in this loch. On a calm, warm day, the whole surface is alive with its bellings, which one would imagine proceeded from so many springs at the bottom. It rises to any colour and size of insect employed, repeating a false snatch until pricked with the barb of the hook. Its dart, however, is not so rapid as that of the trout, and scarcely so true. The char of Loch Achilty generally measures from six to nine inches. It is shaped like the gurnet, and, in proportion to its length, is of small depth and circumference. The head and upper parts are of a greyish-brown colour, marked with whitish spots; the belly and lower fins pink, approaching to carmine. At table it is a perfect dainty, having a fine, delicate flavour, superior to that of any trout I ever tasted. One might easily capture three dozen of them among twice as many trout on a favourable day in Loch Achilty.

Besides the char and trout, this beautiful lake teems with another fish of smaller dimensions, and seemingly a variety of the stickle-back. It swims sometimes in shoals, like the minnow, and sometimes alone. Although no doubt occasionally devoured by the trout and char, I never observed any attacks made upon it by these fish, and am inclined to believe that it is by no means a favourite food of theirs; yet I cannot affirm that I actually investigated this matter with any degree of care or curiosity. Be that as it may, the stickle-back of Loch Achilty is itself a singular production, differing in its habits and appearance from the more common varieties of that little fish. It is thick and girthy, prefers swimming in places of considerable depth, although close to the margin, and moves at a sort of jerking but by no means rapid pace. It loves also to congregate in an unsuspicious and familiar manner round the legs of the wader, exhibiting a sort of stupid tameness that not a little surprised me. There seems to be no regular season for the spawn of this diminutive animal. I observed it paired off both during summer and winter along the shallows, in order to deposit its ova. When in this ripe state, it presents a dull and unhealthy appearance, and its movements were evidently painful and constrained.

The spawning of the Loch Achilty char seemed to me, in several instances, if not in all, a subterraneous operation, carried on among the roots of springs, and in the oozy and caverned outlet of its waters. The fish, I am credibly informed, have been caught repeatedly by means of a creel, during winter, in places where the effluent current, after finding its way some hundred yards under ground, emerged again into daylight, before discharging itself by other subterraneous channels into the Rasay or Black-water, a considerable stream in the neighbourhood. That the char of Loch Achilty do not, at least in any quantity, ascend its feeders to spawn, I am convinced, for I have examined these carefully the whole of the autumn, winter, and spring months, and for some time during sum-

mer, without being able to discover any traces what-
ever of the fish. It is possible, indeed, that they carry
on nocturnal operations along a piece of shoal ground
lying at what may be termed the foot of the loch, opposite Craigdarroch, although I never had the fortune
to observe a single straggler during daylight on the
spot I mention; indeed, the occupation of it by a large
and voracious species of Canadian water-fowl prevents
entirely the intrusion of small fish over this part of
Loch Achilty.

### THE RIVER CONAN, LOCH LUICHART, ETC.

Not far from this lake runs the Conan, a deep and
dark-coloured river, passing in its higher channels
through a number of excellent trouting lochs. Were it
not for the cruive fishings near its mouth, Conan would
no doubt prove a favourite stream with the angler. The
falls also, a short way below Loch Luichart, are a great
obstacle to the progress of salmon, which, were they removed, might proceed inland above thirty miles, and
over a succession of spawning beds of a first-rate quality.

It has been in the contemplation of those interested
in the fishings of this river to blast or cut out a
stair-case channel through the bed of rock forming
the principal fall, and I have no doubt, were this done,
the salmon would immediately take advantage of the
improvement. The same experiment might be tried
at the Rogie falls on the Black-water, a tributary of

the Conan. Of course, scene-hunters and lovers of the picturesque would, and with some degree of justice, place their interdict upon such proceedings. The destruction of a beautiful cascade is certainly a piece of Gothicism quite out of character with the spirit of a polite age, and I would join sincerely with them in deprecating the unhallowed act, were I not convinced that effect might be given to the plan on foot without detriment to the scenic attractions connected with either of the waterfalls. At any rate, ample compensation is made for petty injuries, by the introduction of the salmon through a chain of mountain rocks, unequalled in their wildness, and into the higher parts of a river possessed, as the Conan along Strath-Bran is, with every requisite which could occasion and further the increase of this noble fish.

Both falls—those of Conan and Rogie—merit the curiosity of the tourist. The former are of a savage sort, and the body of water launching itself over the naked rocks is of huge compactness, foamy and turbulent. The approach to it is not the best, and we believe it is seldom visited, although nowise in a very secluded situation, lying about a mile above Little Scatwell. Notwithstanding that it is of very considerable height, more so than an ordinary salmon-leap, a fish occasionally has been known to get the better of it. One was taken, not long since, at the head of Loch Luichart, in a very weakly and exhausted state. Rogie falls on the Black-water are much more frequently ascended than those of Conan, being lower, and having on one side of them a detached run, over the precipitate part of which salmon can easily toss themselves when the river is in any degree flooded. A cruive, however, is placed during the open season at the bottom of this passage.

There is a good deal of picturesque beauty about the Rogie falls, but they scarcely equal those of Conan. On one side of them wave graceful birch-trees, of natural growth; the other is what may be termed a bare ascent, although covered with heather and furze-bushes, broom and juniper. The Black-water is a first-rate angling stream, being ascended by the larger proportion of fish that find their way over the cruives at Conan mouth. The part of it immediately below the falls is rocky, and contains some choice water for the rod. Besides salmon, some portions of it contain beautiful yellow trout, weighing in general from one to five pounds. These may be taken with the fly, but more easily with a small par, although pike are apt too frequently to interfere with this bait. I once caught four trout of betwixt three or four pounds weight each, a short way above the Rogie falls, while trolling with wire tackle and the upper half of a smaller fish. These fellows did not display much cunning, but darted voraciously at the mangled lure, assailing it with the eagerness of a shark, and by no means uninclined to repeat a false bolt, although evidently pricked and cautioned to their heart's content, as I at first imagined. It was plain they were perfectly unacquainted with the shadow of a rod, and never until that day had been taught the mysteries of honest old Isaac. Peace be to their manes!

There are few trout in the lower parts of Conan so large, which is owing perhaps to the constant sifting of its principal streams for salmon. I have occasionally, however, taken them above a pound weight in places inaccessible to the drag-net. Along Strath-Bran also, after the river leaves Ledgowan Loch, and a short way above Achnanault, great fish are to be met with in some of the deep pools. They will rise at a large, red professor-fly, and even grilse hooks have been found effectual. I would much, however, prefer angling there with a small fish upon swivel tackle. Gimp also should be used, to prevent pike, which are very numerous in that district, from doing mischief to the apparatus. Loch Luichart, through which Conan runs, is of good repute as an angling loch; perhaps, indeed, it is somewhat over-rated. The trout found in it averages from half a pound to a pound in weight; occasionally, however, it has been caught of a much larger size. It is a beautiful and strong fish, with salmon-coloured flesh, and magnificently spotted on the outside, but rises to the fly lazily and with great caution, at times merely approaching your hook, and retiring again without so much as a single snatch. I have killed, angling from the side, betwixt three or four dozen in the course of a forenoon with a red professor of the ordinary size.

The streams running into Conan below Loch Luichart are, besides the Rasay or Black-water, the Meig from Strath-Conan, and, lower down, the Orrin.   I am not acquainted with any prime salmon pools on the Meig, except those in the neighbourhood of Scatwell, and immediately below a rocky and dangerous pass, over which the fish only occasionally find a transit. The trout in this stream are generally insignificant, as also are those found in Orrin, although we believe well-sized ones are now and then to be captured in the upper parts of both waters.

Immediately above Loch Luichart, the Gradie river falls into Conan, issuing from Loch Fannich, a considerable extent of water.—Loch Fannich contains numbers of small trout, and possibly a few of great size.   It is, however, scarcely worthy of the angler's attention, being situated in a wild, pastoral, unaccommodating district, and not readily approached even by the pedestrian.   The Strath-Bran lakes, although frequently angled on, and some of them stored with pike, are infinitely superior.

Besides these, a small tarn, lying upon the hill-path betwixt Scatwell and Achnanault, is by no means to be overlooked.   There are twain together, but I allude to the more northernly; for although angling in both, I failed to discover fish in the other.

In fact, I take to myself the merit of being the first who ever drew trout out of this one, and I had failed doing so, were it not for a fit of perseverance which came upon me at the time, for I cannot affirm that the fish are exceedingly numerous, or inclined to bite well, yet they are large, and so singularly beautiful and well-formed, that I defy any loch in the kingdom to produce their equal.    I caught only three of them, with the red professor, upon a Limerick hook.    The biggest of these weighed seven pounds, and measured somewhat about twenty-two inches.    Its girth, when compared with its proportions, was enormous, and its head no bigger than a walnut.    On the breast, it had the colour, and to my fancy the fragrance also, of a water-lily, only that there was a tinge of the rose in its nature.    Farther up, the body became of a light olive colour, gloriously starred over with orange spots. He fought with great spirit, and sprang out of water like a new-run grilse at the end of his first heat, and when obliged to succumb, did so with all the unwillingness of an expiring Ministry!    At table, I never saw even a salmon redder in the flesh, which was interlayered with curd of marrowy flavour and unequalled whiteness.    The other two fish were of the same description, only much smaller, not weighing above a pound and a half each.

Reverting to the Strath-Bran lochs, the angler, a short way from the bridge at Grugie, where there is a public-house, comes, pursuing his way up the Conan, to Loch Cullen. The trout in this sheet of water are some of them of great size; many, however, are under twelve inches in length, but there are few very small ones. I killed one there weighing three pounds, on the same day that I caught the large one mentioned above, besides several others. But I did not handle the rod with much enthusiasm or for any length of time, as it was then getting late and no breeze on the water; besides, I was over-content with what I had already taken. The Cullen trout, judging from the specimens captured by myself, wants both beauty of form as well as fleshy fairness. My largest fish, although not half the heaviness, was almost of the same length as the one previously alluded to from the hill-loch, and its head fully three times the size. The smaller ones, from a pound weight and down-wards, were better proportioned, but by no means beautiful in appearance.

Achnanault Loch lies immediately above Cullen, and is somewhat of the same description, although I have heard it asserted that the trout therein are of larger size and less plentiful in number, pike being very abundant. The cursory trial I took of it showed in a manner the reverse; for of the two fish I captured there in the course of ten minutes, both were smaller than any I caught in the other loch. This, however, arose possibly from accident; indeed, I have generally remarked, when two lakes are near each other and joined by a run of water, that the uppermost contains the larger fish.

Conan above Achnanault, where there is an excellent
inn, runs over a channelly bottom, favourable to the
spawning of trout, which, however, are not quite so
plentiful as one would naturally expect. This arises
partly from the depredations of their enemies, the pike,
partly from the cannibalism of the giants of their own
species, and perhaps also from the long-continued descent of snow-water into Conan during spring and the
early part of summer. There are, however, in many of
the pools heavy and well-conditioned fish. These wink
at a small fly, and love better the bushy and bearded
lure, or else a spinning bait worth darting after, that
gleams across them when the water is quick and swollen.

A mile or two above Achnanault, the Conan
leaves Loch Gowan, a sheet of water of no very
great extent, but celebrated above all others in Ross-
shire for the size of the trout it affords. These
weigh generally from three to ten pounds. I cannot say with accuracy whether any heavier ones
have been captured. I suspect not a great number,
for the range of water is by no means extensive—a
mere pool in size compared with Loch Awe or Shin
—and the fish is evidently not the *salmo ferox*, but
a lake trout of inferior description, differing from it
both in its shape and general features. Like all
large trout, it has certain feeding hours, dependent
frequently upon the state of the weather, but for the
most part regularly timed off by sun and shade.
During these only it can be taken, either by a dark

grilse fly, or by trolling with a small fish. The fly, I believe, is preferable, there being numbers of pike to snap at a spinning bait.

At no great distance from Ledgowan, and in the neighbourhood of Auchnasheen, lies Loch Roshk, a considerable sheet of water, affording very superior angling. Its trout, like those in the places already mentioned, attain to a large size, and may be captured by a good angler in considerable numbers.

I am not personally acquainted with many other lochs worthy of recommendation in the eastern districts of Ross-shire. There are, it is true, Lochs Garve or Malaing, through which the Black-water runs, Ussie and Kinellan, near Strathpeffer, all of which contain quantities of pike; and as to Loch Garve, and a smaller sheet of water in its vicinity, they boast of some good trout, but these are scarcely worth wasting our patience upon, being so dull and capricious. The inky nature of the water which they inhabit seems indeed to injure their appetite for the fly. Perhaps there is no stream in Scotland so dark in its colour, during summer, as the Black-river. Such, in fact, is its quality in this respect, that salmon ascending it have been known to become perfectly foul-hued in the course of forty hours.

Such is the substance of a communication made to the club by one of its members, regarding some of the waters in Easter Ross-shire. No mention, we perceive, is made of Loch Moir, lying at the extremity of Wyvis,

9

neither of Monar in Strath-Orrin, both of which are well spoken of by such as have visited them. The adjoining very brief extracts from another epistolary paper, offered to the inspection of Mr. Wandle-weir, are perhaps worthy of perusal, relating as they do to the more prominent waters in the western districts of the same shire.

### WESTERN DISTRICTS OF ROSS-SHIRE.

I HAVE just angled in the Ewe, Gruinyard, Torridon, Carron and Shiel waters, and may safely assert that, taking them in the mass, they stand altogether unrivalled. The Eve, issuing from Loch Maree, and justly celebrated by Sir Humphrey Davy, consists merely of two or three pools, but these of such a quality, that at certain times a couple of skilful rods might load a horse with salmon, grilse, and sea-trout. The fish, however, are capricious, and refuse to rise during particular states of the water, which, owing to the influence of the wind on Loch Maree, is constantly varying. The loch itself affords what may, in that district, be termed poor angling. The salmon find their way into it with some difficulty, and yellow trout, though occasionally to be met with, are by no means very abundant. Char, resembling those of Windermere, inhabit its deep places, but are not to be captured with the fly. The scenery is grandly wild, yet scarcely so savage as that on the banks of the Torridon, which present to the eye a continued surface of loose and scattered rocks, singularly arranged, and prodigious as to quantity. I found this latter water in a very exhausted state, and consequently met with little success. I am informed, however, that, when flooded, the angling is very superior. I was more fortunate by many degrees on the Carron, the lower pools of which being in prime condition, and full of fish, afforded me as fine sport as I ever before experienced. Had I been provided with good tackle, I might easily have mastered above a hundred weight of salmon and grilses. As it was, having only a trouting-wand, and slenderly-dressed flies, the execution made by me among the larger sorts of fish was greatly limited, and I had chiefly to content myself with the demolition of some scores of sea-trout and finnocks. The former of these gave excellent play, being fresh-run and generally well-sized, averaging from one to three pounds in weight.

There are several fresh-water lochs in the district of Loch Carron, but I cannot greatly commend them, save that they are somewhat picturesque. Salmon which have surmounted the cruive-dyke above New-Kelso are, however, occasionally to be caught in the lowermost.

Passing to Loch Alsh, and from thence to Loch Duich, a beautiful and superbly wooded arm of the sea, I fell in with the Croe and Shiel waters, both of which, when in a flooded state, are reckoned excellent. My success at the mouth of the latter was fair, but by no means equalled what I met with on

the Carron. I had, however, a store of fish in my
creel, and trudged on with a contented heart towards
Cluany, from which next morning I angled my way
through Glen-Garry to Fort-Augustus.

# CHAPTER VIII.

## ANGLING TOUR

### TO THE NORTH-WEST HIGHLANDS.

EARLY in the month of August 183——, Messrs. Leister, Otter, Swiveltop, and May-fly, as was their wont during summer, set forth on an angling expedition to the North-west Highlands. The route selected by these gentlemen differed in some respects from that taken by Wandle-weir and his friends, who were probably by this time on their return southwards. A communication from Mr. Herl-broke, dated 25th July, had been received by the club at C——h, previous to starting, wherein he stated their success, considering the dryness of the season, to have been of a satisfactory nature ; only three salmon, however, had as yet been captured, the reduced state of the streams confining their amusement, in a great measure, to angling in lochs and hill-tarns.

Mr. Leister and his companions were fortunately not destined to experience the calamity complained of by their English brethren. On the contrary, their very outset was conducted under a beautiful discharge of the watery element; and on arriving at Loch Awe, where it was intended their operations should commence, it proved to one and all of our anglers a matter of no little gratification to discover the Orchy and other surrounding waters desirably flooded and trimmed out for sport. A large salmon was quickly taken by Tom Otter, above the kirk at Dalmally, and Jack Leister was so far successful as to load his pannier to the lid with honest-sized trout. Nothing, however, worthy of notice was achieved either by May-fly or the worthy Doctor, who, it may be remarked, went to work in an indolent, leisurely, and over-presumptuous style, without deeming it worth their patience to exercise any degree of craft or ability,

The day following was spent by all four in trolling from a boat for the *salmo ferox*, of which redoubtable species of fish they had the misfortune to lose three fine specimens, securing only a sorry individual of five pound weight, along with a score or so of excellent yellow trout, averaging in their length from twelve to fifteen inches. The escape of the larger fish was owing principally to the intervention of a strong variety of water-weed, along the nettings of which the boat at the time of their seizing the bait happened to be directed. To this subaqueous retreat the trout, on

finding themselves hooked, naturally retired, and, en-
tangling the cordlines by which they were held among
a series of lengthy roots and inextricable cables, gave
to our anglers no other choice than that of parting
company with them, which, as this act of submission was more than twice repeated, had the effect of
calling forth many sore expressions of temporary
regret.

We have no intention, however, of following out
the movements of our piscatorial adventurers further
than is detailed in course of the annexed conversations,
which, linked though they be with little incident, may
nevertheless prove worthy of a hasty perusal.

### GLEN ETIVE.

*Enter* MAY-FLY *and* SWIVELTOP.

*May.* Stretch thy wits, good Doctor, a hair's length.
I am sorely nonplussed, and confoundedly knocked
up. Oh! this weary trudging o'er moss and moor,
through strong chasms and torrent beds—this wrest-
ling with hunger, rain, wind, and darkness—it takes
the romance out of one for ever! Where, in the
name of wonder, is this track they talked of, and
the precious domicile yclept an inn?—eight miles

off!—ay, and eight twice told; which, with our morning's walk to boot, is no small matter. We have been sixteen hours agog, Doctor—I don't bate a minute—and no cheer at our lips neither.

*Swivel.* Keep up heart, Bill, we're in old Scotland still, and by a stream-side.

*May.* Plague on the stream! Now that you talk on't, these fish on my back are not feathers.

*Swivel.* Toss them to the ravens, Bill—no marvel thy courage is low under such a burden.

*May.* Art thou serious, Doctor?—is it in thy philosophy to separate us from our spoils? Thou hast broad shoulders; prithee carry them awhile, and exchange panniers.

*Swivel.* Ay, Bill, with wondrous satisfaction.—Is all to thy mind? [*Exchange baskets.*]

*May.* Even so.

*Swivel.* And to mine also, Bill. [*Drops May-fly's fish among the heather.*] This load steadies me, and puts vigour into my limbs. I can now resist the wind, and plant my foot with more firmness on the heath.

*May.* I wish thee all joy of such blessings, Doctor. But where are we, and why advance? What a wilderness I can fancy around me!—hills, mosses, and decayed forests. This glimmer is more frightful than utter darkness—I like it not. The stone-blind night hath fewer horrors. Ha! what is yon?

*Swivel.* A white ghost to be sure! Maybe, Bill, 'tis the ghost of the inn we are searching after.

No lights, however—no merry fires to draw the damp out of us! But stay—it moves.

*May.* Ay! Doctor, so it doth. Gra'mercy, 'tis a wraith!

*Swivel.* If so, by all means let us capture it; 'twill make our fortunes, Bill. A show-spectre will charm the virtuosi, and reduce the over-stock of men's wits. Mayhap 'tis one of Fingal's heroes! We are not far from Cona, mind you—and if such, what tales it may unfold? How the tomes of learned antiquaries will slide from the glass-case to the lumber-room, when their pure palaver is exposed and contradicted by its legendary tongue? But how shall we bribe it to approach, Bill? Shall. we offer it thy trout, man?—wandering ghosts are always hungry.—But ha! it moves again.

*May.* Let us pass quietly to this side—

*Swivel.* And flee our good fortune?—Nay, Bill, nay, thou advisest without judgment. I will show my front, and question it as to our track and destination—where this King's-house on the moor of Rannoch lies.

*May.* Folly! perilous folly!—but take thy way on't, Doctor.

*Swivel.* Oh! by all the miracles of St. Anthony! 'tis a horse—a cart-horse—and nothing but a cart-horse! Hie thee, Bill, this way, and behold a cart-horse.

*May.* No unwelcome omen, Doctor;—the inn cannot be far distant.

*Swivel.* But how are we to find it, Bill ? Is't to the right or left hand of us, think you ?

*May.* To the left, I opine.

*Swivel.* To the left, then, let us turn by all means, although I have my doubts on't.

*May.* Doubters are always in the wrong, Doctor.

*Swivel.* We shall see, Bill. I marvel much what Otter and Leister can be about at present ?

*May.* Snug at Bunaw, where we ourselves ought to have remained, instead of trudging up this houseless glen without their company, and at dead of night too —ay ! and hungry as wolves, wet as fishes, and weary as souls in purgatory.

*Swivel.* Who is to blame, Bill ?

*May,* Oh ! of course, my unfortunate self. But what could we miserable anglers capture out of the broad Awe ?—not even a wretched par.

*Swivel.* And what *did* we capture out of the narrow Etive ?—Where were the hosts of sea-trout you promised me, Bill ?—the sparkling salmon and capering grilses ? Where that pleasant inn your fancy pictured, overlooking a pool paved with fish, so that from its windows we might handle our wands, and while discussing the contents of a punch-bowl, land at the same time a sixteen-pounder ?—Glorious dreams, these—Elysian visions, Bill ! What a brief walk we had, besides, from Portsonachan, level and void of roughnesses ;—to be sure our eyes were well feasted ; there were heaths, and brackens, and barked trees in abundance, and heads of hills besides, rather grand-looking, but to my taste very unsocial and grim-visaged. I fancy a green, southern, flowery knoll before any of them.

*May.* Tasteless impiety! thou'rt a monster of prejudice, Doctor.

*Swivel.* So be it! But how shall we turn now? the river, you perceive, takes an angle, and should we pursue it on towards the source, 'twill only bewilder us the farther.

*May.* Then, Doctor, I must drop. Should the inn be not at hand, 'tis useless to goad me on, I am past remedy, and can take my chance upon the wet heather until sun-rise.

*Swivel.* Out on thee! thou art not so flagged, Bill; give me back my pannier. We must ford the stream; 'tis impossible that the King's-house lies on this side on't. There is neither road nor foot-path—and road, of a certainty, there ought to be, or Scotland is not Scotland.

*May.* I protest against such daring. The river is swollen and rapid as a race-horse; we shall be carried off in a twinkling and never again heard of. Many of the pools are whole fathoms deep.—There's peril in't, even in day-light—but now—

*Swivel.* Be brave, Bill, be brave. I'll pick thee a passage, man, will not over-whelm thee. Strangle these Gorgons of thine, and follow me. See you, the river is not greatly flooded, and this is no doubt a shallow stream, although somewhat rough and noisy. I shall feel my way with my rod. Not knee-deep, Bill, I affirm!—Come on, boldly—ha! there's a slippery stone hereabouts—push to the left.

*May.* I shall be down to a certainty.

*Swivel.* Keep thy legs together, and thy side to the current—move! move!—deliberation is danger. See, I am nearly across. Thy hand, Bill—we are safe!

*May.* 'Tis well, for I am sadly worsted; and now let us rest an hour on this bank.

*Swivel.* Not one minute; I value my life more. 'Twould stiffen us to do so into sheer corses. Up, up, Bill! and shake the drench water off thee by a brisk gallop towards yon dark-looking object a short way before us. 'Tis a hut, but an uninhabited one—a goat shed, methinks. But hurra! here is the road—the government road leading to Fort-William! We are close upon King's-house, Bill!

*May.* I see it not—and yet, as you say, it must be at hand. How shall we proceed, Doctor? right or left?

*Swivel.* I am puzzled, Bill, like thyself. 'Tis certain, however, that Glencoe lies in the latter direction; should we take the other we stumble upon Rannoch moor, where, for ought I know, we may stand at this moment. Let us decide by the toss of a coin; heads, right—tails, left.

*May.* Tails!

*Swivel.* To the left then we go—

*May.* And on a good, smooth road, which 'tis a

pleasure to travel, after the rough bone-shaking we
have just had.   I feel wonderfully recruited, and able
to perform miracles.

*Swivel.* Vaunt not, Bill; but take thine own creel,
an' thou be'est so valour-getting.   These trout of thine
annoy my shoulders not a little.

*May.* Ah! Doctor, art thou failing at last?   But
hand the pannier this way—why, it seems to me like
an air-bladder!

*Swivel.* So it ought, Bill, seeing its contents are one
and the same.

*May.* What! hast thou made away with my fish?
Audacity indeed! unexampled sacrilege!—flung what I
have toiled and sweated for to the base-born carrion-
crows?   'Tis too much to endure meekly.   Doctor
Swiveltop! I abjure thy fellowship.   Thou art a common cateran and body-spoiler.   Away! away! lest I
inflict the bastinado, and pommel thee into shivers.

*Swivel.* Most valiant May-fly! we honour thy very
infirmities.   Be not wroth as the roused lion, nor slay
us in the heat of thine anger!—What to thee, Bill, are
a few score of fingerlings?

*May.* Fingerlings!   Doctor Swiveltop?—they were
pounders—ay, two pounders!

*Swivel.* Oh! Bill, not a two-ounce fish amongst
them.   'Twas an absolute sin in thee to butcher such
fry.   Saw you not how the very swallows, while thou
wert swinging them out, pounced upon them instead of
gad-flies?

*May.* I assert, Doctor Nathan Swiveltop, that those trout of mine, you so wilfully and criminally abandoned, and which you now most slanderously hold up to ridicule, were, one and all of them, large and delectable fish—that they weighed in general from two to three pounds, although, at the same time, I will to any one, save yourself, allow that five or six of the smallest did not greatly exceed nineteen or twenty ounces.

*Swivel.* Good !—excellent !—bravo !—well-done !— hurra !—and thou wouldest have forced me, Bill, to carry thy pannier, containing five dozen such fish (far beyond a hundred weight, mark you), for the pure sake of displaying thy prowess to the ignorant inmates of a country inn, and without any regard or fellow-feeling for my fatigue and endurance ?  Methinks I did well to rid me of such a load !  Egad, Bill, thou art a vile computer and wretched arithmetician.  This paltry fabric of willows, yclept thy creel, may barely contain a stone-weight of fish, yet, to thy fable-making fancy, 'twould conceal leviathans.  O ! how thou stretchest the borders of nature to make room for unheard-of marvels !

*May.* Hold thy prating, Nathan Swiveltop, and anger me not.

*Swivel.* Thy wrath is pleasant, Bill—pleasant as comedy.  I love thee when fired, and hate thee when cool.  I love all passionate men.  The even-tempered, and what some term the amiable, are either villains, cunning, selfish, and avaricious—otherwise they are

fools, silly, simpering, and inanimate.   But here, heaven
be thanked, Bill! is a turf-hovel—and inhabited, I presume.   Let us arouse the slumbering Celts, and make
enquiries as to the inn. *(Knocking.)* Ho! good folks, hollo!

*May.* Hit harder, Doctor; apply the butt-end of thy
rod to this make-shift of a door.   Hear you that
flourish of nose-trumpets!   What a snorting these
sleepy-pates make!   Hollo! bestir ye!   *(Knocks.)*

*Swivel.* Thou hast thunder in thy fists, Bill, like old
Jupiter; but these worthy souls seem charm-bound,
quite entranced—hollo! you, hollo!

*May.* Ha! they move and hold consultation.   Can
you direct us to King's-house, honest folks ?—*(No
answer.)* Hollo! you inside! have you tongue-pieces or
ear caverns?—speak for the sake of mercy—we are
lost wayfarers, tired as tinkers' mules, and hungry as
trapped weasels. *(Another whispering.)*

*Swivel.* They take us for burglars or cut-throats.
We are now in Glencoe, methinks, and the massacre is
not out of memory!

*May.* Give them a touch of Gaelic, Doctor; quote
Ossian, or shout a war-cry.

*Swivel.* Alas! Bill, I am a poor scholar, and know
not the lingo.   Up, knaves, and show face instanter?
Uncourteous hounds! why lag ye on your straw, while
two wandering knights of the angle crave their way to
the hostelry?—Up, ye lazy loons!

*(Voice from within.)* Her nain sel pe comin—what
does she want with Alister Mactonal'?

*Swivel.* Why, the road to King's-house, good Alister.

*Voice.* Ta Sassenach is on ta road.

*Swivel.* Ay ! but on which hand does it lie ?—east or west ? north or south ? up or down ? right or left ?—Dost thou hear, Alister Macdonald ?

*May.* The fellow has slunk off to bed. Hollo ! . Alister Macdonald—son of a dog ! show thyself—come forth, Alister, come forth.

*Voice.* What does ta Sassenach want ?

*May.* Thy face, rascal. Do you take us for gaugers ? Ajar with that gateway of thine, and give us a peep at thee.

*(Alister, cautiously opening the door.)* Ta man be good, and her face pe good.

*Swivel.* Better than her heart!—And now, Alister Macdonald, tell us, I pray thee, where we are—Is this Glencoe?

*Alister.* To pe shure.

*Swivel.* And how far may we be from King's-house ? —a mile ?

*Alister.* To pe shure.

*Swivel.* Six miles ?

*Alister.* To pe shure.

*May.* The man is a dolt—let us on, Doctor !

*Swivel.* He is a knave, Bill. Stay—dost thou know what this is, Alister ? *(Displays his purse.)*

*Alister.* Ta siller, to be shure.

*Swivel.* Well, tuck thy kilt on, and be our guide to King's-house ; we will reward thee like princes.

*Alister.* And what will ta Sassenach gi'e to her nain sel' ?

*Swivel.* Make an honest demand, Alister.

*Alister.* Twa guineas frae sic shentlemans, shure enough ?

*Swivel.* Get thee to bed, greedy hound !—thou shalt not see a doit of mine.   Away, bare-faced, lazy-boned rascal ! we have no need of thee.   Put wind into thy sporran, and make a bagpipe o't.   Come along, Bill, and leave that boor to learn modesty.

*(Alister Macdonald shuts the door, muttering a curse in Gaelic.)*

*May.* Another specimen of these western Celts ! —rude, abject, and rapacious.   They have neither conscience nor good-feeling.   Marked you how that miserable wretch shook with sheer terror, as he displayed himself cautiously at the entrance of his hovel, after the long colloquy held with his helpmate under the blankets, during which, I have no doubt, they both convinced themselves of our intention to rob and murder them ?

*Swivel.* Very likely, Bill, but we must now retrace our steps ; for the inn, I feel assured, lies not in this direction, and as for obtaining a night's lodgings elsewhere, 'tis out of all likelihood, judging from the reception we have just met with.   Quick march, Bill ! —what ails thee, thou man of valour ?

*May.* What ails a wind-broken horse or a jaded hound ?   I am desperately flagged, Doctor, quite

10

knocked up; I can't drag a leg after its fellow, I can't lift a jaw, or turn a cheek, or throw up an eye-shutter. My back aches, my belly groans, my legs totter, and my hands are weak and passive as an infant's.

*Swivel.* This is a sudden change. Methought thy vigour was restored, and that thou wert fresh as at starting. Where now hath thy valour gone, that I may bring it thee? But move, man, move! Force up courage for a score of minutes. Shake thy machinery into action.

*May.* Nay, Doctor, I cannot. I am conquered for want of thews invincible; I have walked off all power of walking on—my heart halts and——

*Swivel.* Fudge! But thou art ill-like in earnest, and chalk-coloured in the visage. Mount upon my back, Bill; I will carry thee, man; come, get up.

*May.* Not so, not so; let me lean on this stone awhile. 'Twill revive me, Doctor, and freshen my limbs.

*Swivel.* Folly! hoist thyself on these shoulders of mine. Thou art light as thine own pannier, and salmon-sized withal. Fancy a stirrup, Bill, and put thy foot in't. I am no restive unruly charger, but sure-paced, and quiet as a lamb. So mount thee, Bill—necessity has no law—besides, thou hast the joke to thyself.

*May.* I will e'en ascend thee, thou biped perilous! —but not fast, not fast; for I am giddy as a windmill, and the wits are flying out of me in legions. Be thine amble gentle and measured, as thou wert a lady's palfrey and no war-horse. Methought I saw a light—and there again!

*Swivel.* Some marsh-lanthorn or Will o' Wisp.

*May.* Nay, Doctor, nay; lift thy head and opine on't. Is't this King's-house, think you?

*Swivel.* A haunted cairn, Bill, and a witch at her cantrips.

*May.* 'Tis the inn, Doctor, I wager a round sum. Halt, and let me dismount ere I am jostled to death.

*Swivel.* Thou art a poor equestrian, Bill—but look! there be two figures approaching us from the stream side.

*May.* Heaven defend us!—move quicker.

*Swivel.* O thou craven!—where are thy ails and heart-burns? How gottest thou wings in such a hurry? Speed, speed, speed!—the Celts are after thee, Bill! (*May-fly exit.*) What hath seized the fool, and who are here to harm him? Do none walk i' th' night save cut-throats? O white-liver! what cost is't to resemble a man, and by an assumption of courage hold his attitude, albeit having no more o' the true virtue in thee than a mouse's hide. Were there not twain of us besides, should they prove dishonest? An air of common resolution would have scared them. But these are no night marauders. Ha! ha! ha! Otter and Jack Leister.

*Enter* OTTER *and* LEISTER.

*Leister.* Even so, Doctor. What dost thou here?

thy creel on thy back moreover? Where is May-fly?

*Swivel.* Saw you not how he fled, terror-struck, at your approach? 'Tis plain he is no hero. His misapprehensions converted you into highwaymen, and I doubt not he will have reached the inn by this time, should these be its walls from which yonder light proceeds.

*Otter.* How, Doctor, still in search of your night's shelter? We thought to have found you snugly seated by a good fire, merry about the face, and in that sort of agreeable semi-slumber which refuses all power of locomotion to him who is seized with it.

*Swivel.* And you envied us mightily, Tom, no doubt. Ah! to your fancy, we came off easily, after being thrice drenched, bogged, and bewildered. I might fabricate a winter's-night tale out of our disasters, did I so design; but you are laden, like elephants—ha! here is a salmon.

*Leister.* Ay, and three grilses—a *salmo ferox*, and eleven sea-trout. These are only part of our day's sport. The remainder, however, which we left at Bunaw, were chiefly yellow-fry and finnocks. Our *salmo ferox*, as you see, is on Otter's shoulders, and weighs sixteen pounds. He is a rarely-formed fish, and was taken with the Maule-fly at the outlet of Loch Awe. But you shall have him to scrutinize at leisure, when we reach the inn. How got you on at the Etive, Doctor? Did May-fly fulfil his vaunts?

*Swivel.* Question himself, Jack.—See, there he is *in propria persona*, attended by a Celtic body-guard, for the purpose, I imagine, of delivering me from the hands of such notorious highwaymen and slayers of the king's lieges, as you and Tom Otter.

*Otter.* Greet him with three cheers.

*All.* Hurra! hurra! hurra!

*Enter* MAY-FLY, *attended by two others.*

*Swivel.* To the rescue, most valiant Bill! I am sore beset by these foot-pads on either side of me. What? armed with a pitch-fork, too? charge upon them.

*Leister.* Nay, a truce, Master May-fly, we sur-render—mar us not, I pray thee, with a weapon so unseemly.

*May.* Is't thou, Jack, and Otter too? egad! boys, but ye have sprung out of the water, and must have rushed up Etive, like twain milters. Here is the hostelry yclept King's-house, as you see, and here am I, Will May-fly, blind and pinched below the ribs with fatigue and famine; wherefore, haste ye, mas-ters, and enter, so that I may satiate *instanter* the cravings of nature—fill up my internal vacancies, nook and cranny, with such moor dainties as this refuge-roof affords—and forthwith betake myself, plenteously primed, to slumber on cool sheets, all blanketings abjured and discarded.

*Intrant omnes.*

# CHAPTER IX.

## CARRON, ROSS-SHIRE.

### OTTER *and* LEISTER.

*Otter.* I am all in a tremor, Jack, and cannot un-riddle my tackle for want of nerve. See how these flies are bewildered! Here is a Gordian knot with a vengeance, and no remedies beside me but patience and my penknife. The former I have lost, and to it I set with the latter, hacking and maiming this way and that, while you, already trimmed, are on the point of discharging your hook at the snout of one of those gallant fish, which belabour the water with their tails in all quarters. What a muster of salmon, grilses, and sea-trout!

*Leister.* Ay, Tom, and I have hold of a fellow at throw first—a grilse by his capers, five pound weight, and wild as a north-west swirl. He seems as if one shook nettles at his forehead, flinging and floundering without stay or reason. I have captured many that held their death-strife more deliberately. 'Tis in vain, Sir Silverside, that thou art so frolicksome! I have the lead of thee, friend, so shore-in sideways. Now, Tom, take thy turn o' the pool.

*Otter.* Nay, Jack, I will onward or above thee, and may pitch on a stream to my fancy, where the fish are as numerous as they seem hereabouts.

*Leister.* I doubt it; there is no part of the whole water so promising, barring the Cruive pool, which has already been dragged by the fishermen, and of course, besides having been thoroughly disturbed, is pretty well emptied of its contents. No doubt, you may meet with abundance of sea-trout near the mouth of the river, but the salmon and larger fish are chiefly lodged within a hundred yards of us. Set to, Tom, and take the noblest of them in tow. Ha! you raised a huge fellow, but neglected to strike. Change your fly for a smaller one, and cast higher up.

*Otter.* I shall bide by my hook, Jack; 'tis faultless. There again——a different fish——

*Leister.* And missed him, too! I would cause my fly to move more rapidly over the surface; the fellow rose at it as if suspicious of harm. Send it a sort of galloping pace, and it will smooth down this distrust. Excellent! he springs after it like a tiger. —Line, line, line—line and your legs—a sixteen

pounder—run, Tom—now, wind up like lightning,
—he takes a somerset——

*Otter.* And is off! hook and all—no help; my gut
tackle is single, and by some degrees too weak; I must
use it in plies, or run the risk of parting with every fish
which I may chance to fix.    You need not stand idle,
Jack; lay on amongst them right and left; you are sure
to have hold of a fellow immediately, only use caution in
guiding him, and disturb the water as little as possible.

*Leister.* I shall certainly keep on guard against
doing so.    What plunges these monsters are taking!
But there is no use throwing my fly over them, they
have not appetite for it at present, and are merely
diverting themselves; yet there be some less capricious spirits awaiting me underneath, which keep their
frolics in check until quickened by the taste of my
steel barb.    One showed face at me this instant, and
leaves a vortex on the water behind him—again he
has risen, and with no better result.    I shall put on
a lively looking Irish fly in exchange for this dull
insect, and should it not ruffle his gorget, I abjure
further intermeddling with him.

*Otter.* No mighty threat this, Jack.    I have now
armed my line with a stout Maule-fly of moderate
size, and have no doubt it will banish the lethargy
out of some half-dormant epicure, and cause his flanks
to turn over magnificently on the gravel.    Already
I have fastened on one of Neptune's ambassadors
to the river-gods, a splendid salmon, excelling the

one I have just lost. See how he posts across the pool! But what! are you similarly occupied with another of the retinue?

*Leister.* I am, Tom; and 'tis a gallant fin. Who shall conquer first?

*Otter.* My rod is a degree too slender, and I cannot deal as is meet with this fellow. It bends almost to my wrist, and is in danger of giving way immediately should he make any violent efforts to escape. But he is too heavy to throw himself out of the water with readiness, and seems inclined to steer deep rather than vault and gambol on the surface. I shall find it difficult to fatigue him, as I dare not trust to this switch of mine, and his leisurely saunterings up and down the pool are no small proof of inherent strength. That fish of yours seems in a fair way of subduing himself by over exertion.

*Leister.* He is an active fellow, and, were not my wand a double-handed one, might manage to give me the slip; but I hold him firm, and have no fear of his flinging off. I have already taken much of the devil out of him, and he now begins to show rib and turn up his keel despondingly. But no! he is out again, marring the reserve of the pool, as if there were fire at his tail. Should I get him into shoal water, I must have the gaff-hook employed *instanter*—and yet without assistance, 'tis no easy matter to run it across his flanks. Hilloa! boy, can I trust you to take the keeping of this rod into your hands a moment, while

I lodge my grappling iron in the body of yonder
salmon ?　Hold tight, my youngster, here he comes,
twelve good pounds I warrant him.

*Otter.* The fish I have hold of is still heavier, and
flags a degree or two in the main, but I shall have
some work yet ere he is thoroughly tired out.　His
paces are more measured and sober, and he seems not
a little non-plussed how to proceed.　The curbing of a
prime salmon like this is pleasurable to our nerves.　I
like his runs and rangings—his zealous pushes after
escape and liberty—his strong facing of the rapids,
and his plunge brave and systematic.　Help him to a
touch of thy gaff-hook, Jack, and, mind thou, keep
clear of the line, and do the job cleverly, as thou art
wont.　Good ! he is mastered ; lay him alongside of
the other, and let us test the twain, while the pool is
under process of recovery.　The floundering of these
fish must have scared their neighbours ;—but no, they
are still at play, and, if tempted cunningly, will show
face to us anon.　The salt-water louse is still on the
pate of this fellow ; he has but lately left the sea, and
is in beautiful trim for the table.　Shall we pack him
off to the inn, Jack, and have him cooked for our
dinner ?

*Leister.* Nay, Tom, I love to be graced with my
spoils, and were you to rob me of their presence, 'tis
ten to one but I should lose all power and inclination
to take another cast.　Allow them to remain, I shall
angle the more vigorously when they are by me.

What is this ? no other than a lively fresh-run sea-trout.

*Otter.* A boisterous rollicker, Jack, agile as Harlequin ; tame him, tame him.

*Leister.* 'Tis pretty sport getting hold of such merry ones ; he is sport, however, and must ashore without further ado, else he will aid in rousing his comrades to suspect our propinquity. That was a good salmon you struck at, Tom.

*Otter.* Ay, but he is clear off, with the bite of a Limerick, on his tongue-end. Marry ! he will bethink himself well ere he venture again after fly-food. I have taught him to be sapient.

*Leister.* A rare spot this for fish, Tom. Look you here what famous fellows are still holding *gaudeamus !* —but 'tis no use marching my hook over them, they are too saucy to raise a nostril towards me, save in sheer contempt of my skill and feather-craft. Methinks we should abandon the pool for an hour or two, and go seawards after the white-trout and finnocks. We have thrashed the water hereabouts to our heart's content, and are not likely to evoke aught more of the monstrous out of it at present. So e'en let us proceed.

*Otter.* You advise justly, Jack, but first we may as well make a change in our tackle. I shall append a black-professor and one of my own grasshoppers. 'Tis killing, as you know, among sea-trout. The boy will carry our fish.

ANOTHER PART OF THE WATER.

*Leister.* Count your spoils, Tom, muster up your booties; 'tis time for us to be steering towards our night quarters. I am somewhat voracious, and my rod-arm is waxing stiff. Besides, what further is't possible to achieve? the breeze is dead, and the fish dull. 'Tis now past four in the afternoon, and we have plied at it these eight hours, doing, it must be granted, no small damage. Let me see, I have here twain salmon, five grilses, and twenty-nine sea-trout, along with a score of finnocks and burn-fish.

*Otter.* Good! you out-weigh me, I fear, but not greatly. I have but one salmon, four grilses, thirty-two sea-trout, and about a dozen or so of the other trash. Scarcely are they to be carried homewards, methinks, by these tired arms and aching shoulders. 'Tis a herculean load after its sort, and fortunate we are in not having to travel any distance. Wet thy lips at my flask, Jack, 'twill help thee to strength, and annihilate the seeds rheumatic, which a day's cold wading is apt to imbed in the soil of one's constitution.

*Leister.* Thy medicine, Otter, hath an honest look; better is't, of a verity, than most stuffs and liquids. They are fools that cry out on't, as it were alway harm's maker, though used at need-time and in moderate measures. Prime whisky 'tis, that hath tricked scrutiny and baffled the gauger, having the breath of the heather and the spirit of the grain, welled out in silence by the tarn-side. Dark forms watched at its birth; the eagle and the red-deer were in their trust; and up at midnight, like a ghost of the mountain, rose the small smoke of their secret fire.

*Otter.* What, Jack! whisky eulogies!—ahem! poetic too! Oh! tush, man, tush!

*Exeunt.*

# CHAPTER X.

## ADVENTURES.

*Enter* MAY-FLY *and* SWIVELTOP.

*May.* Let us down upon earth's lap, good Doctor, and take note of the prospect below us. Of what use is't to tramp onward in rear of Jack Leister, for the purpose of persecuting a few loch-trout? Have we not laboured already, enough and in vain? I am cowed out of patience by heat and gad-flies. Oh! for the cold descent of some winter-spirit, to fan off in his flight these stinging sun-rays. Art thou not in a thaw, Doctor? dropping apace?

*Swivel.* Ay! verily, Bill; but here is a tree-trunk, old, girthy, and wizard-like, yet withal green in part, and offering kind, cool shelter to our exhausted limbs. Let us throw ourselves down beneath its shadow. 'Tis an alder—and such an alder! There are other trees of like size in its neighbourhood. What trees ¡

they rival England's eldest oaks—not in height, I
allow, but in circumference of stem; perhaps in age
also. See these knotted congers and hideous constric-
tors—the writhing and athletic mass of disinterred
roots. Are they not worth our contemplating? Here,
Bill, let us drop.

*May.* What! among these ferns, and in the proximity
of this ant-hill? I love not the offensive crawlers,
nor consider my flesh safe in their neighbourhood.
They are a bandit brood, and infest the bracken-forest
far and wide. Rather let us ascend to yonder jut of
gray rock, from which the bearded goat hath just now
sprung; 'tis more to my mind as a resting-place, and is
sheltered also by another of these alders, fully as large
and fantastic as the one which you first admired.

*Swivel.* We are both of us bad selectors of a lux-
urious seat. If you dread ants, I am no friend to a
rough, hard, and uneasy stone-crag, when it may be
avoided by our progressing to yonder patch of smooth,
dry verdure, the very spot which a wood-nymph would
select for her summer couch. It is both sunned and
shaded, and see, from its ferny marge, upstart two
gentle roes, wild, beautiful creatures—children of a
dream. They are not altogether afraid, but pause and
turn to gaze with large, mild eye, on our intrud-
ing presence. Who that saw them now could be
their butcher?

*May.* I would not trust even thyself, Doctor, wert
thou aptly armed. 'Tis bad sensibility, and mawkish

to compassionate a prime roe-buck because of his big eyes and graceful attitudes. I sympathize none with it. But the twain are gone, and have no faith in thee, despite of thy pitying phrase. Howbeit, thou hast pitched upon a pretty covert for our day-slumbers. The turf is to a wish, soft, green, and free from damp; and these birches, though they want the architectural build and amplitude of the trees we have left in our rear, form a cool, pleasant screen, such as we much desire to ward off from us the sun's oppression. Let us rest our rods athwart this bough. Have they not a picturesque and natural look about them, as if they were things of growth, not of handicraft? This is true luxury, Doctor—more so than wading waist-deep for a nibble.

*Swivel.* Allowed, Bill;—but I have still an eye river-ward, and fondle the notion of some huge, black trout inhabiting yonder deep, half-sluggish pool. Yet as for starting them now under such a sun, 'tis impossible. I am content to imagine their existence, and should I be led to angle again in this quarter, may have the good fortune to take prisoners a creelful. At present let them enjoy life untempted.

*May.* Even so;—the sights and sounds on all sides of us are infinitely more attractive to me than the cutting off of their brief careers. Hear you not the falls at this distance? how this continuous murmur haunts the air, intermingled with the more lively brawling of the stream below! What various musics hath nature, and with how much of nicety do they suit humanity—ay, and operate on the heart, moulding its moods and tempers according as they are high or low, solemn or humorous, glad or terrific! The voice of such a waterfall speaks home to our feelings, and separates from the servile flesh, where they are inhumed, those loftier portions of our nature, that are akin to the Maker and God of good. Among Scottish cataracts, Doctor, I would reckon this of C———n not the least imposing. 'Tis in no wise hackneyed or hurt by tasteless artifice, like many of greater note, yet hath it all the sublimer characteristics of these. The body of water is strong and straitly confined, descending vigorously over a rampart of high rocks. 'Tis a gallant and terrible leap, as of a whole legion into a pool of wrath — and alway in front arises a spray-spectre, taking its form from the winds. You may mark it from where we recline, but not so clearly as to distinguish the rainbows with which it is inlaid.

*Swivel.* To tell thee my mind, Bill, I am no mighty admirer of waterfalls. Should they be well reputed and praisingly talked of my fancy is apt to exaggerate their attractions, and when visiting them I ever become disappointed. Yet such a cascade as this, stumbled upon unexpectedly, fails not to arrest my attention. There are no violations of nature throughout its confines—no foot-print of the Goth within the sanctuary; all is secret as where the hinds calve.

11

What see we around but huge hills, bare and bleak—
or skirted, like this one, with promiscuous wood—
and below us, to our left, only a single stripe of
plough-turned soil, with a few scattered hovels, each
of which is tenanted to the full by the children's
children of such as were centuries past the inhabiters
of the self-same spot? These are no intruders on
solitude, for they hum ever close to their own hives,
and adventure not in quest of sights and sounds, remote
but a step from the roofs under which they harbour.
Despite of them build within call the boding raven
and the sun-buzzard, while the red-deer of Achilty
brandishes his careless antlers from rock and forest.
Listen thou, and spell out the elements of nature's
anthem—the dulcet clusters of glad voices, that fill
the surrounding air. Bees, birds, and waters, mingle
together their several harmonies, and now, among these
thousand twinkling leaves above us, singeth plaintively
the summer wind. Its tones unman me most, for they
are soft and touching as of female sorrow—yet this
gust is bolder, Bill, and creates a crave in me to test
again the water. I must up and away to the loch of
Herons above Tarvie wood, where I may chance,
should the breeze improve, to ring the snouts of a
score as spirited fish as ever cleft flood—and that
in spite of all threat or restriction on the part of the
proprietor.

*May.* This is a sudden resolution, Doctor — a
wayward caprice. I am in no mood to second thee,

but shall slumber pleasantly where I am, until Leister heave up alongside, on his return from Loch Luichart.

*Swivel.* The ravens will assail thee, Bill, an thou sleepest; moreover, there be wild cats in the neighbourhood, and weasels without count. See, what is this?—no other than a huge viper.

*May.* Say you, Doctor, a viper! a hydra! Egad 'tis time to shove off—where is the legless ruffian, that we may smite him?

*Swivel.* Here, Bill, coiled up like a Russian knout, and hissing on us with head erect, after the fashion of a tea-kettle. He will escape an you be not quick at marring him.

*May.* No fear; I shall stay his careering stylishly, or the cunning is out of my right hand. Marry! I have hit him on the sconce, and ta'en the edge out of his fangs; but I must now impede his motion with a tail-cut, else will he, as you say, bid us good-morrow among the brackens. How lovest thou this, thou worm of Acheron? methinks thy vertebral screw is somewhat damaged! Oh! thou ugly, flat-pated fiend, toad-hued, abominable reptile, still wouldest thou exalt thee with grim malicious visage and horrid crest! Abate thee, Master Spitfire, and bite the sod!

*Swivel.* What bloody fractions, Bill, thou hast parcelled him into! Where is thy heart, man? Beshrew thee for want of charity!

*May.* Bah! Doctor, 'twas in sheer charity I so

malefactored him. Were he not vile in his nature
and dangerous, I had as lief let him free. As 'twas,
he got but a semi-torturing. But start you or stay?
—In truth, I myself have no relish for further down-
sitting, seeing 'tis at such peril as these ambushed
adders cause to one's breech. Nay! to speak truth,
I have an inkling after merry sport in this loch you
talk of, and though inclined to be sluggish, shall
nevertheless shake myself, out of courtesy, into an
active humour.

*Exeunt.*


### HERON LOCH.

*May.* The little waves are riding forth by hosts. I
like well the water's aspect. See you, there be some
fellows on the feed at the distance of three rods.
Let us lay our lines over them. 'Gad! what a
vault this copper-fin took; but the barb is in his
tongue, and he may whistle a death-dirge. By Jove!
'tis a very cayman in vigour!—he runs line like a
salmon, and——

*Swivel.* Is off, Bill.

*May.* Ay, Doctor, sped and away! gone by the
spirit of mischief! My courage is down ten degrees
at a start.

*Swivel.* Faith! 'tis true; what a melancholy attitude you are in! Cheer up, Bill; one would imagine
you were become bankrupt, and had a surcoat out
at the elbows—in fact, that you meditate self-

destruction—and all for loss of a twelve-inch trout, the like of which may be taken at next cast by one of moderate skill and even in the temper.

*May.* Is't so, Doctor ? then I'll to't again. Marry ! as you predicate, I have seamed another at the muzzle, and no stripling—but I must use caution, for he makes towards the bottom, where the weeds are dense.— Hallo ! knave, astir and shun trickery—fight fair, master trout !

*Swivel.* So, to my mind, he doth ; not being on parole, he is free to escape when and how he listeth.

*May.* I have him.

*Swivel.* You have, Bill ! O conquest unparalleled ! triumph without equal ! never within its ribbed confines throbbed, like thine, the big heart of some king-subduer—never was so stirred the pride of orator, when he held in the chains of eloquence a thousand listeners —all naturally freemen ! Come, be not too large in thine own reckoning ; lower thyself a grade out of charity, lest I be terror-struck in thy presence, Bill, and lose valour. Howbeit, I am nigh on a level with thee, and hold fast some lively water-cleaver, which mayhap is destined immediately to bite the marge. But who is this making towards us, Bill ?

*May.* Marry ! I know not. He hath a boorish gait —but is armed, one may perceive, with authority. No doubt he intends to act the mar-sport. What say you, Doctor, shall we resist, or move off quietly at his bidding ?

*Swivel.* Resist, by all means, Bill. There can be no legal hindrance to our angling hereabout, seeing we possess freedom of trespass from the tenantry. Are trout not common to all, and the property of the captor ? Let us combat the matter, Bill, and stand fast.

*Enter* KEEPER.

*Keeper.* May I ask, masters, whether you have the proprietor's written permission to angle in this loch ?

*Swivel.* How, friend, does your laird shut up his waters, so that strangers, like us, have it not in our power to take an hour's amusement even on a remote hill-top ? We have no passport, nor count upon one as needful, but intend to remain where we are, until driven away by the strong hand ; wherefore attempt not of thyself to foil us, but betake thee else-ward.

*Keeper.* Having warned you, masters, you will not refuse to yield me your names for prosecution, else must I proceed to call in assistance, being so empowered ?

*Swivel.* Here be our cards, friend, which you may bear on a thunderbolt to your laird ; meanwhile, we shall angle here according to our discretion, and shall possibly, you can inform him, do ourselves the honour of presenting him, ere sunset, with a creelful of good trout—so God speed you ! —What wait you for ?

*Keeper.* To say truth, masters, you will find it better to be advised.

*Swivel.* Oh ! we are in no such humour, and shall abide the issue with great content ; again, I pray you, depart, an you bear love to your master.

*Exit* KEEPER.

*May.* The fellow hath a look expectant, and moves snailishly on his errand.

*Swivel.* Ay ! he gapes after a bribe, and would fain wink at our breach of his laird's ordinance ; but what is rightfully ours we design not to purchase, so e'en let him wag his tongue against us ; 'tis to me a matter of moonshine.

*May.* Set to, Doctor, now that we are quit of the knave, and fill up thy pannier. 'Twill astonish Leister, should we out-weigh him, as we might do with a little management. There is a deep piece of water eastward of the heronry, to which I would fain repair, while you thrash on hereabout.

*Swivel.* I am content to do so, Bill, having promise before me of good sport.

### ANOTHER PART OF THE LOCH.

*Swivel.* What, Bill, seated disconsolate on a stone, waiting like cock o' the weather for a wind-puff ! Are thy flies still in sallying mood ? Hast had luck, boy, that thou'rt so patient grown ?

*May.* I have tooth-ached not a few rascals, but

the greater part were too nimble for me, and fought themselves off the hook ere I could enforce their submission. Out on them! they are tender-mouthed, yet strong in the tail and of ample muscle, else had I encreeled a neat score of them. See, the seven I have slaughtered make of themselves an honest heap, and might stand in room of an eight-pound slice of salmon. But where, Doctor, hast thou been? I have missed thee from the water's edge these two hours, yet seemingly art thou well-laden with fish, if fish these be on thy shoulders, causing thee such uneasiness.

*Swivel.* Ay, that they are! two and three pounders each! I captured them in a small tarn lying not three hundred yards from where we stand, yclept Loch L——n. 'Twas signified to me by an urchin I chanced to fall in with, immediately after your departure; and although somewhat incredulous of his information, I determined, as it lay at no great distance, to give myself the benefit of a trial. The trout, such as I have taken from it, seem to have been planted there some years ago, and are by no means numerous. In fact, I question much whether they have as yet spawned, notwithstanding the facilities they have of doing so; there being several small water-courses running into various parts of the loch. I have mastered thirteen of them, and, strange to say, these were all I encountered; but they rose with great truth and avidity, and were mostly hooked in the throat or lower part of the tongue, so that, without any very great exertion, it was impossible for them to escape, my tackle being strong and in good order.

*May.* How, think you, they weigh?

*Swivel.* Two stone at the least, not an ounce under. They are no bagatelle you will allow, and pain my shoulders considerably—the strap of my pannier being somewhat narrow. I will relieve myself for a space, and lay out my spoils on the heather.

*May.* What a swasher has this been!—gaunt and big in the bone, a contrast rare to that sleek-sided monk of a fish you threw just down, which more resembles one of those caught in this loch, save that it hath twice its dimensions, and is of darker hue about the belly;—altogether, you have wrought an achievement, which will cause Leister to 'rub his eyes out of suspicion that they are sadly bewitched. Faith! but I shall forth myself, an it please you to guide me, and make second mischief among the knaves.

*Swivel.* Nay, Bill, not in such haste; 'tis a dead calm on the water surface. Moreover, methinks I have mastered all such as were within reach of my fly and in rising humour. Delay till to-morrow, and may you speed well!

*May.* I shall task myself to do so, seeing your counsel hath reason in't. Do you not marvel, Doctor, at the heronry on yonder islet? What a singular aspect it presents! Not a leaf is there on the whole cluster of trees, where are cradled the huge nests of the fisher-bird, but bare they stand, as if under the thraldom of winter, and disarrayed by the tempest. 'Tis, at such a season as this, a strange sight, out of accordance with all summer things.

*Swivel.* But not so, Bill, with nature. From her treasure-house of wonders she ever instructs us, foiling her blooms with barrenness, and, in the centre of what most rejoices, exhibiting a wreck like this, to remind us of frosts, winters, and decay. There is something impressive in the aspect of those rude fabrics, reared by unwieldy birds, and repaired by them with religious diligence, as if they were indeed very sanctuaries. And so too they are, for in them have been cradled many generations of the heron-tribe. Through antiquity they have become sacred, and sacred moreover are they, as domestic abodes—retreats for the young, the wearied, and the blood-bestained. Hearken to the clangour of their many inhabitants ! the various notes and signal-cries with which they fill the air. One might imagine a military encampment not far off, and these sounds to be martial ones. See, there is a heron-patriarch, wheeling above the others—a slow air-pacer, with white crest and plumage. He is a bird of authority, and, as he lowers himself towards the islet, all in the garrulous divan become quiet.

*May.* Let us swim across, Doctor, and indulge ourselves in a narrow inspection of this curiosity.

*Swivel.* With all my heart, Bill. I wish we could send a truce flag before us, and cause these long-shanked islanders to know of our pacific intentions ; however, at the worst, we shall only scare them during a brief interval from their domiciles, and this, methinks, is no great grievance. What, Bill, already on the point of plunging ? Have a care of those water-weeds to your right. They are tough and long, and should you strike in amongst them 'twill be no easy matter, I apprehend, to escape perdition. But stay ; let us start together. I would fain back my oars against thine for a handful of groats. Now, push off.

### THE HERON ISLE.

*May.* Manifestly, we are intruders, and, to speak truth, Doctor, I am alarmed lest a bold bird or twain from among these screamers should take heart to attack us. We have no weapons of defence, and by these beaks overhead run risk of being stilettoed at a swoop. Good luck ! here is a cudgel, and a strong one.

*Swivel.* Folly, Bill ! Art afraid, man, of a few water-fowl ?

*May.* Not so, Doctor, but I stand on guard, being ignorant of their natures. Marry ! are they not threatening in their attitudes, wrathful in their cries, dangerously armed, and desperately congregated ? But, what have you there ?

*Swivel.* An unfledged bird, which I am somewhat at a loss how to capture, he employs his rostrum to such good purpose. However, I have got my fingers about his throat, and shall lug him into your presence.

*May.* 'Sooth, a strange-looking object! Think you he would prove delicate at the fork's point? 'Tis a prize, Doctor, and must visit the mainland in our company. He will roast trimly, despite of these stilts of his.

*Swivel.* Aback! pitiless epicure—is this thy humour? Came we here as kidnappers, forsooth? Why tarry these birds that they enact not the harpy upon thee, O destroyer of their progeny, and violator of their cradles? But it must not be, Master May-fly, and this scion of theirs I shall hoist again into his nursery forthwith.

*May.* Truly, he merits no such favour. Look at this pile of bone, scale, and refuse. What gluttons he and his kin are! 'Tis their usage to make a pretty havoc hereabout among the infant fry. They are poachers consummate, and do more to depopulate our salmon rivers than the whole of our fraternity. Let us make an example, and gibbet this bird at the threshold of his sires.

*Swivel.* Most monstrous and unchristian! I credit not my ears, Master May-fly. Is such truly thy proposition?

*May.* Even so.

*Swivel.* Thou'rt cool withal—singularly cool. Can'st

take a scalp, Bill, or sever a windpipe, or brew broth of vipers? Art up to all the sleights and trickeries? Stars! I have a perilous neighbourhood, and walk on thorns. Where gettest thou thy lack of clemency, Bill? Is't framed or natural? purchased or gifted? Hath it limits? or is it in extension infinite? But come—at length off thine eyebrows is the grim resolve; thou art driven to be compunctious.

*May.* Not a whit;—to appease thee, however, I am content to forego the committal of an act so thoroughly barbarous as the neck-screwing of a young heron. Now—may we recross, an it pleases you.

*Swivel.* With much good-will.

### SIDE OF THE HERON LOCH.

*Swivel.* Array thee in haste, Bill; I espy yonder our morning friend the keeper bearing down upon us in company with two other mongrels of like stamp or calling.

*May.* E'en let them pass—

*Swivel.* If so they list, but such is not their design. Mark you how the rascals will make law for us without warrant or commission. Their whole aim is to usurp our angling-rods, but they may save their cunning, else have I, Nathan Swiveltop, lost stance for my wits.

*Enter* KEEPERS.

*1st Keeper.* So ho! masters, still as I left you?

*Swivel.* Nay, friend; my rod is idle, as half an eye might discern.   This is a fair piece of water.

*1st Keeper.* And I warrant me, you have raked it foully.   But you must e'en deliver these rods and fish into our keeping, and trudge off.

*Swivel.* Hear you, Bill, what the knave hath need of!   I presume, friend, you hold special authority for this demand.   Well! should we decline compliance, how mean you to act?   What! is't thus?   Aback and discover your warrant, else shall we reckon with you as common foot-pads.   I pray you, hands off!—is it your design to assault and rob us?   'Sooth, ye should have studied your men more accurately—but take a care.

*2d Keeper.* D—— you, sir, yield up this rod!

> *2d* KEEPER *attempts to seize the fishing-rod from* SWIVELTOP, *who knocks him down.*

*Swivel.* Art satisfied, friend?—By heavens! rascal, lower that barrel of thine.

*1st Keeper.* Surrender by G—!

> *Presenting his gun, which* MAY-FLY, *rushing up to him, forces out of his hand, and flings into the loch.*

*May.* Eh? villain, wouldest play the miscreant? March thou after that birding-piece of thine, and allow us to pass. Gad, Doctor, yonder comes Jack Leister at full speed.

*Swivel.* And in the nick of time—Ho! master keeper, no slinking! an thou goest, carry thy gun with thee; 'tis within reach, and will pop out splendid bilge-water. Art pettish, forsooth? stay then, and file in with thy comrades. Marry! we shall find law to redress us, seeing you have been handled so smoothly. Assault with intent of robbery!—'tis no light offence, mark you!

*1st Keeper.* We had the laird's orders.

*Swivel.* Your laird's order, friend!—what! to plunder us of our property, and, in case of resistance, level a barrel at our heads? Who is this laird of yours that is so absolute? By Jove! he hath rare power now-a-days, that can frame his own statutes! But go your ways, and learn to give the laws reverence. Were we so minded, you might find this matter one of some cost. Well, Jack, whence come you?

*Exeunt* KEEPERS.


*Enter* LEISTER.

*Leister.* Across from Loch Luichart, with intent to take a cast hereabouts on my way to the inn. But what has happened, Doctor?

*Swivel.* Only a tussle with some of the laird's keepers, the particulars of which I shall recount to thee on our road homeward. How has it fared with thee, Jack, in the way of sport?

*Leister.* By no means as I expected. I have about nine pounds weight of fish slung over my left shoulder, and these earned by sheer dint of perseverance, without help of breeze or cloud. Is it by otter-craft you procured such a burden, Doctor? Uncover, I prithee, and give me the benefit of an in-peep.

*Swivel.* Immediately, Jack; but first let us on a space, and baffle the eyes of these three knaves who have just quitted us. 'Tis want of policy to allow them knowledge of our good fortune.

*Exeunt.*

# CHAPTER XI.

## CLOSE OF THE SEASON——NOVEMBER——FISHING WITH SALMON-ROE.

### MAY-FLY *and* OTTER.

*May.* 'Tis yellow November; and on apace creeps chills and storms, those calamities among which the year closes. Methinks there is a mood o' the mind to every month in the calendar——and now, 'tis our month of melancholy. Let us hang up the wand, Tom, until spring-tide. I have lost my love to it a degree or two, and feel as if nature for a season were wresting it from my hands. How hastily the dark waters glide, leaf strewn, as it were by the fingers of fairy foresters! They have too mournful a hue for our flies, and not a trout can one note at the surface.

*Otter.* I design angling, Bill, with the salmon-roe, of which I have a store in my creel. See, there are Leis-

12

ter and Swiveltop doing execution therewith on the stream immediately above us. That trite saying, " the more the merrier," holds good of this sort of water-raking. Wherefore let us set to—they will join us ere long, should we have pitched upon the better pool. Shorten your line, Bill, and throw up against the current. A large single hook you may, on the whole, find preferable to the double ones you have in your pocketbook; however, try them, they will retain the bait more readily than the other, but are scarcely so well adapted for securing the fish. I feel already the rub of a snout against my barb; and now I have one fast, a good yellow fin, and not a whit out of season, judging by his complexion. Fix a leaden pellet or twain, four inches above the hook, Bill, and while angling, keep your casting-line more on the stretch. Tug smarter, man; you would scarcely run your point through a fungus at that rate of striking. I have another, and shall capture half a score besides, ere you draw blood.

*May.* The fault is in the fish, Tom, they bite with such delicacy and want of vigour.

*Otter.* 'Tis their manner, Bill, when feeding on this bait, to suck it like the carp—but less hesitatingly than you imagine. I mistake much if it be not frequently engrossed within the jaws of a huge fellow, without our being able to perceive the slightest indication of an attack made upon it. The true secret of roe-fishing is in fact to strike immediately upon the progress of the

hook appearing in any degree checked, and not defer
doing so until we sustain a direct and palpable assault.
But you employ too large a bait, and compress it arti-
ficially round your wire, like a soap-ball, designed to
cleanse the outside rather than tickle the palate.   A
bit the size of a horse-bean is sufficient ;—and note you,
Bill, allow it to cling to the steel-barb, as you naturally
remove it on your finger-point from the jar which contains it.—But I have hold of something huge ; 'tis a
sea-trout methinks, black, lubberly, and impotent.   He
wallops down the river without half his ordinary
strength, and can with difficulty draw out a fathom of
line from my reel.   I pity the poor fellow, and should
I land him, shall suffer him to escape.   He is of no
account out of his element save as manure ; even
crows would pick lazily at him !

*May.* Toss him to me, Tom, he will aid wonderfully
the filling of my pannier.

*Otter.* Nay, nay ; 'tis a fish forbidden, and must
off out of sight in a twinkling.   There are water
bailiffs about the place, that no doubt keep eye upon
us ;—moreover, I have a certain strong respect for
the close-season, and am unwilling to violate the
enactments relating to it by the detention even of
a paltry finnock.

*May.* This sounds well ; but, faith ! 'tis somewhat
questionable.   I had rather trust gold with a knave
than a goodly salmon with thee, Master Otter, be the
day of his capture when it might.   Were not this a

lank kipper, of woe-begone aspect, beshrew me an thou
would'st have parted with him so readily!

*Otter.* I grant you, Bill, you have reason for your
conjecture.   There is strange magic, I allow, in the eye
of a clean-run salmon, which one hath just uncoffined
from the pool where he designed wintering.   I could
no more resist it than Adam could the apples of our
grand-progenitrix.   Yet with respect to ripe, pregnant,
and unwholesome fish, I aver that the meddling therewith is a disgrace to our craft, who ought, above all
others, to be the natural protectors of the spawner, and
favour, to their utmost ability, the increase of salmon.

*May.* Neat professions these, were they alway acted
up to.   But how comes it, Tom, that your mighty
regard for the close-season allows you to break in upon
it as you do at present?   See you nothing injurious to
the breeding of these noble fish in our angling for
trout among their places of resort, and over the very
channels where they are accustomed to shed their *ova*?

*Otter.* Much otherwise.   There is no species of
enemy so hostile to the salmon while spawning as
the common yellow trout, a single individual of which
will consume, in the course of a day, nearly its
own bulk in roe.   You may perceive, by the readiness with which they assail our baits, how deadly
they are to the unhatched progeny; and truly
we can do no greater service to the holders of sal-
mon-fishings on the lower parts of the waters than by
thinning the swarms of spoilers, which at this period

hover around the pregnant fish. These, in order to obtain the dainty meal, rake up the gravel in all directions, and scruple not to devour promiscuously the roe and fry of their own species. I have now hold of a voracious-looking rascal, and shall discover to you the contents of his wallet. Is not this an offender of note ?—here is no less than an ounce of newly shed spawn, mingled sparingly with flies and water-insects.

*May.* He hath paid the penalty. But look you, Tom, how Jack Leister and Swiveltop bring in the bald-pates. If, as you say, the more the merrier, what objection have you to dip a hand into the mine of their good fortune ?

*Otter.* None in the world, Bill.

# CHAPTER XII.

## SCENE, A CHURCH-YARD.

*Enter* LEISTER, OTTER, SWIVELTOP, *and* MAY-FLY.

*May.* Here let us wind up and unscrew. What is more fitting than that we close the feats of the year in a church-yard ? Ah ! Doctor, we are out of all humour with Time, he hath put to flight so many schemes of ours. Designed we not more than the summer hath room for ? and now where is even the smoke of our intentions ? But 'tis better in truth as it is, else were there too many remembrances of happiness in our hearts not to make the future miserable. I like to find that disappointments have been mingled up with pleasures, it steels me the more against suffering. And this has been the last of the year's anglings, Doctor ; I am sorry for it and yet glad !

*Swivel.* Well do I comprehend thee, Bill, for sorrow and gladness are in me also, blended into that affection which men call melancholy ;—perhaps 'tis the place we stand in that awakens it,—this fastness, of which, saith one,

> " In the valley of life is the garden of death,
> Mourner on mourner entereth
> That Eden of woe, and on its sward
> Layeth the burden of his regard.
> Mourner on mourner ! another train
> Bringeth the earlier back again ;
> They have chosen his home, and borne his bier,
> And watered his turf with a human tear.

> " It is a strange and solemn spot !
> Friendship, and faith, and feeling, forgot !
> Folly findeth wisdom there,
> Walking the tombs with a sombre air ;
> And awed into thought are the giddy, and they
> That have fostered pride fling the bantling away."

What epitaph, Otter, are you and Leister decyphering ?

*Otter.* That of an honest man and an angler, one of the old members of our fraternity.

*May.* Peace be to his ashes !

*Otter.* Amen ! Bill. I knew the old man well ; he was my earliest instructor in the gentle art ! You remember him, Leister, when we were yet boys, how he loved us. I have his rod still, and a sterling piece of wood hath it been in its own time.

There are notches on't, along its butt, denoting the length of great fish mastered by the skill of its first possessor. I can recall, through means of these, many of the venerable man's exploits, as related to us by his own lips in the days of our childhood. Now that I think on't, the pool we have lately been angling upon was a prime favourite of his, and I hold some recollections, too, of aiding him at the landing of a huge salmon among yonder shallows. Yes, Jack, 'tis a dream of yesterday. I have the kind eyes of the aged angler beaming upon me, as I attempt to carry in my arms the ponderous fish ; he relieves me silently of the burden—silently !—the familiar spectre cannot speak ! there is no voice in the visions of memory !

*Leister.* How rapidly, Tom, fleets the mind over the thousand links that connect it with the past, and with what mysterious power it enters into the hermetic chambers of Time ! Well hath one said, " There is no such thing as forgetfulness !" Standing here, I could recount the tale of my boyhood—those little plots of which it was formed, until now lost sight of, even by myself.

*May.* The angler's grave ! What associations it presents of one that hath trodden the vales of his native land—of a lover of peace, poetry, and the poor—of him who lived in contentment, and died——

*Otter.* Not on his bed, Bill. My ancient friend, Mr. Brigstanes, fell a martyr to his angling enthusiasm, and was drowned, aged seventy-one, at a swollen ford on the river Clyde. It was nature's way of taking him from the world, and could scarcely be termed a death of violence. Another of our fraternity lies buried in this very church-yard; but the head-stone, owing to some accident or other, has been removed, and I know not the exact turf under which he sleeps. Nor is it of much matter; he has lain nigh half a century, and there is nought in the treasure-house of our memories whereby to call up in his behalf a single, solitary regret. Some brief verses, which now glance across my recollection, relative to the death of one of our fraternity, you will allow me on this fitting occasion to repeat.

### The Angler's Grave.

I.

Sorrow! sorrow!—bring it green;
    True tears make the grass to grow;
And the grief of the good, I ween,
    Is grateful to him that sleeps below.
Strew sweet flowers, free of blight;
    Blossoms gathered in the dew;
Should they wither before night,
    Flowers and blossoms bring anew.

II.

Sorrow! sorrow!—speed away
    To our angler's quiet mound;
With the old pilgrim, twilight gray,
    Enter thou on the holy ground.

Here he sleeps, whose heart was twined
　　With wild stream and wandering burn ;
Wooer of the western wind,
　　Watcher of the April morn.

III.

Sorrow at the poor man's hearth !
　　Sorrow at the hall of pride !
Honour waits at the grave of worth,
　　And high and low stand side by side !
Brother angler, slumber on !
　　Haply thou shalt wave the wand,
When the tide of time is gone,
　　In some far and happy land.


### BURNING OR WATER-FORAY——BLACK-FISHING.

*May.* Let us leave this spot, Jack. The look on't
lowers my spirits, and the dismal moaning which these
ash-trees make hath an effect on me which I love
not to encourage.

*Leister.* I have no wish to remain here any longer,
Bill, and 'tis meet we should forthwith be on the start.
There is a rumour afloat of a burning to be held to-
night on the Meikle-water. Intend you to be present,
Tom ?

*Otter.* Nay, Jack, I have no great relish for this
illegal sport. It is both cruel and irrational, and
harms immensely the increase of salmon. As for the
spearing of healthy fish during the open-season, and in
daylight, as I have seen practised with the single hand

on some waters, I say nought against it, seeing it requires like skill and perseverance as angling with the rod does ;—but what is there needed of these virtues, in order to strike a row of steel prongs into the ribs of a dormant spawner, lying with exposed fin in the narrow of a mere brook, especially when those engaged in the employment are a numerous band, and in use to surround the pool with their persons as with a net, giving no chance of escape even to a solitary straggler ? 'Tis in truth a barbarous pastime, pursued more for sake of the fish, black and unwholesome as they be, than out of frolic and amusement.

*Leister.* You are somewhat severe in your conclusions. Be persuaded, however, to join us for one night, and, believe me, you will abandon your present opinions with respect to this mode of salmon-fishing.

*Otter.* In truth, I have but little wish to act the beholder of your intended massacre, and might be tempted, were I to accompany you, to offer some measure of interference ; more, in fact, than I could enforce with safety to my person.

*Leister.* You are not altogether so rash, Tom ; our poor old friend Brigstanes, who now lies here, would, as you well-know, have been among the foremost in a ploy of this nature.

*Otter.* No doubt, no doubt; and for his sake, I shall resolve to join you.——What say you, Doctor ?

*Swivel.* I am already bound to show face.

*Leister.* So is Bill here.

*Otter.* Faith ! we are a posse of pretty scoundrels, and merit well the pillory for our intentions ; ne'er-theless, we shall not draw back in the matter.

*Exeunt.*

We possess no lengthened record of the black-fishing alluded to in the above conversation. It seems, however, that Tom Otter took no inactive share in the proceedings of the evening, and actually slaughtered with his own hand a trio of huge kippers, much to the satisfaction of his friend Leister ; who thenceforward prided himself not a little in having vanquished so effectually the scruples of his brother angler. The burning, or water-foray, as it may appro-priately be termed, proved on the whole a successful one. Seventy fish, salmon, bull-trout, and grilses, bit the shore ; yet, strange to say, so monstrous and sinful a butchery elicited no further comment from the late traducer of the spear-system, than—" 'tis a marvel the simple fools knew not their element better !" A con-vivial meeting was held by the club on the following evening, which was attended by Leister, Otter, Swivel-top, Gaff, May-fly, and Hackle.

The year was now drawing to a close, and our anglers had resolved to lay aside for a time the im-plements of their craft, and betake themselves reso-lutely to the more serious occupations of life.

A sketch of the farewell feast, devised and participated in on this occasion, is the only remaining fragment we possess relating to the now defunct fraternity at C———h.

The subsequent spring brought along with it to their customary haunts no return of jovial and light-hearted souls.   One member only, save ourselves, of the dispersed brotherhood was beheld traversing the deserted valley.   Over his broad shoulders waved carelessly a long, black wand, the point of which ever and anon caught among the obtruding twigs of a green hazel fence.   Nor did this repeated annoyance seem in the least degree to ruffle the temper of the philosophic angler, who, at the continual recurrence of it, retraced his steps with unaltered patience, in order to extricate his line from the mischievous impediment.   It was our friend Jack Leister.

Jack Leister!  We cannot speak of changes in the melancholy manner they ought to be spoken of, but a certain pressure of our comrade's hand, as we came up to him, denoted that he had not altogether escaped their influence.   The breaking up of the fraternity at C———h had greatly affected him, and it was evident he possessed no degree of appetite for the sport which he almost unconsciously was about to pursue.

But why say more of this our interview—to both of us so sad ?  Why linger over scenes which it were better to close up, lest, opening them afresh, we open the heart with them ?  Ah ! the enthusiasm of those first days, how it has departed! What a fashion hath the reality of the future presented itself in, so different from the resemblances which Hope, the deceiver, led us to rely on! We shall not think of culling flowers out of the quicksand any longer.

# CHAPTER XIII.

## FAREWELL FEAST OF THE ANGLING CLUB.

### LEISTER, OTTER, MAY-FLY, *and* SWIVELTOP.

*May.* Pile high the faggots, Meg; give us an ample, exhilarating flame — an ox-roaster, prithee. Ay! that is the fashion on't; put thy bellows into its ear, and blow right lustily — force a jolly heart into the centre of these fir-logs. Thou art a good girl, and pretty withal, and wilt lack neither mate nor merriment. There is nought, my boys, equal to a prime sparkling fireside. 'Tis, next to his Bible, the poor man's best comfort; and merciless wretches are they who refuse, as many do, the clearings of their coppices to supply the hearths of those needy gleaners, with whom God surrounds them in His mysterious, but just distribution of wealth and of poverty! Without this blessing, how rugged and unsocial were we, kept all apart from those kindly intercourses, which are formed and enlarged within the hallowed semi-circle! His fireside is the true secret of the Briton's strength and superiority, of his intellect, his patriotism, his piety, and the thousand virtues with which he is adorned! Rome, like Britain, long as she flourished, venerated her hearth and household *lares*.

*Swivel.* Give the jug an impulse, Bill, and hearken a stave from Jack Leister. The lilting humour is in his throat, an I guess accurately. Out on this thy practice of thrusting soliloquies across our converse! Is it not better, when a pause is in't, to fill up the occasion with a song? Come, Jack, take the lead.

[LEISTER *sings*.]

**Ø waken, winds, waken!**

I.

O waken, winds, waken! the waters are still,
And silence and sunlight recline on the hill;
The angler is watching, beside the green springs,
For the low, welcome sound of your wandering wings!

II.

His rod is unwielded, his tackle's unfreed,
And the withe-woven pannier lies flung on the mead;
He looks to the lake, through its fane of green trees,
And sighs for the curl of the cool, summer breeze.

III.

Calm-bound is the form of the water-bird fair,
And the spear of the rush stands erect in the air,
And the dragon-fly roams o'er the lily-bed gay,
Where basks the bold pike in a sun-smitten bay.

IV.

O waken, winds, waken ! wherever asleep,
On cloud or dark mountain, or down in the deep ;
The angler is watching, beside the green springs,
For the low, welcome sound of your wandering wings.


*Otter.* There is no need to invoke the elements at
present ; the blast is bitter enough, and with pitiless
anger tears down the beechen draperies inclosing our
retreat.   How it howls, as if through the monstrous
windpipes of many air-fiends ! its very pauses are
parts of the unearthly concert, enacted by some demon
of silence.   I would love none to be belated to-night
on some moor-stretch.

*May.* Nor I, Master Otter.

*Swivel.* As we know well !   Recollect you our trip
to King's-house up Glen Etive ?   Ah ! Bill, who that
saw thee then, and beheld not misery in person ; a
weary, woful, and bewildered wight, famished and
courage-fallen.   But scowl, Master May-fly, with less
unkindness ; neither sharpen thy tongue against me.
Bear with my humours, I pray thee.

*May.* Were I to do so, Doctor, the charity of the
deed would pass without recompence.   Of a verity,
thou deservest the cudgel.

*Swivel.* Confessedly, Master May-fly.

*May.* Albeit I shall rest content with a song.

*Leister.* You usurp, Bill—but agreed.   The penalty
is a fitting one ; so, Doctor, strike up.

13                  .

[SWIVELTOP *sings*.]


## The Yallow-Fins o' Yarrow Dale !


I.

The yallow-fins o' Yarrow dale !
　I kenna whare they're gane tae ;
Were ever troots in Border vale
　Sae comely or sae dainty !


II.

They had baith gowd and spanglit rings,
　Wi' walth o' pearl amang them ;
An' for sweet luve o' the bonny things,
　The heart was laith to wrang them.


III.

But he that angles Yarrow owre,
　Maun changes ever waken ;
Frae our Ladye's Loch to Newark Tower,
　Will find the stream forsaken.


IV.

Forsaken, ilka bank and stane,
　O' a' its troots o' splendour,
Auld Yarrow's left sae lorn and lane,
　Ane scarcely wad hae kenn'd her.


V.

Waes me ! the auncient yallow-fin,
　I marvell whare he's gane tae ;
Was ever troot in Forest rin
　Sae comely or sae dainty !

*Otter.* I had as lief, Doctor, thou hadst left thy stave unsung; it hath troubled the strings of my affections. —Ah! I shall never visit Yarrow any more, not because its breed of yellow-fins is now extinct—and well might they be so—for the waters of that stream have been harrowed without mercy, sifted and ransacked by every species of ingenuity, down from Douglas-burn-foot to the bridge at Broad-meadows, and farther perhaps; but farther we never angled, although often, from Newark Tower to that of the wizard Sir Michael Scott at Oakwood, have we trodden, along the birchen braes of the silvery river. Its yellow-fins are indeed departed!—the huge, thick-shaped, golden-flanked fellows, that were wont to be caught in the May month, during glints of the sun on a warm rainy morning. They loved best the clear, shining minnow, or sometimes a yellow-bodied fly, with a rough red hackle twisted round it; but of these, the minnow was the more captivating lure; it brought out the daintest fish from their retreats, and spun so enchantingly down the primest streams that, troutless as one knew many of these to be, there was still a delight, difficult to forego, in playing among them its tiny form. The Yarrow yellow-fins were ever famous, and an unfrequent specimen may to this day be taken, but only one, out of some scores of gray, lean, loch trout, or of the big-bellied variety found in Tweed. It was, in truth, a lovely fish, ornate with a rare sprinkling of stars, darker than crimson, and these on a light amber ground, which, shaded off towards the belly, became gradually like mother-of-pearl. The head was small, the back curved, and the fins yellow, as a newly minted guinea.

### THE ETTRICK SHEPHERD.

But not for the loss of these is it, that I shall never visit Yarrow any more;—it is because the *genius loci*—the Ettrick Shepherd—has departed! Alas! gentlemen, I have too many angling associations connected with James Hogg, ever to endure again the sight of his favourite Yarrow. Times without number have we traversed its banks together, our slender wands bending alternately with the weight of a struggling trout; and on St. Mary's too, and Loch Skene, and Meggat-water, have we twain fashioned our thoughts and converse to the wild, mystic, unviolated scenery around us. But those thoughts and that converse may not be renewed; from the crushings of the mould there is no rescue, and nature's ordinance cannot be disturbed by any turbulent aspiration of ours.

The Ettrick Shepherd was a singular character— a combination of many virtues with some defects— genius mingled up with its foibles; and these latter the more conspicuous, seeing that no measures were ever put in force to conceal them. In the sphere where most men of talent move, they learn the art of hiding, by a splendid hypocrisy, their other weaknesses. But this art was never understood by James Hogg. He delighted in the broad exposure of his frailties ; and a natural conceit (for such it must be acknowledged he possessed) made him too careless of the censure and advices of others. He hated the trammels of criticism, and disclaimed the sagacious precepts of the lettered inquisitor. Most of his productions were rapidly thrown off—their execution kept pace with their conception ; accordingly, they remain full of crudenesses and contradictions. These defects, however, are overlooked in the fancy and originality of the Shepherd Poet ;—the drossy and faulty surface is concealed among the ignitions of his genius.

For one of the self-taught, Hogg shone wonderfully. His best honours were gathered without the aid of patronage. He climbed the obelisk of fame alone— not that officious advisers kept altogether aloof, but he rebutted with vigour their sacrilegious suggestions. In none of his poetical compositions was the Ettrick Shepherd an imitator of the Ayrshire Ploughman. His songs differ in their fabric and melody from those of Burns. They are wrought of a lighter and more fanciful material, but they want the strength and judgment—the severe beauty of execution—the felicity of thought and language. Among them, however, there are many lovely and soul-stirring ditties, pastoral harmonies, and Arcadian airs. Hogg was a master in rural poetry. He had an eye and heart for all the operations of nature, and reverently did he pro-

gress her domains for wild and beautiful fancies
wherewith to beflower his page. He revived the old,
elfin superstitions of his country—strewed with ideal
structures the valleyed hills, and cast over them a
new mantle of glowing and kindly associations. Much
of what the Ettrick Shepherd has written will continue imperishable, and much also lie entombed with
himself, or, at any rate, remain, as matter of mere
curiosity, whereon may speculate some sage unborn
philosopher, the pride and paragon of a future century.

Hogg, talking of him as the man, not the poet,
was out of his element in society. He appeared to
anything but advantage abroad from his own fireside.
His real character became disguised among follies and
affectations, to which, in his calm and natural mo-
ments he was an utter stranger. To such as knew
him intimately, these feelings had a very different
seeming from what they possessed in the eyes of
others. The latter regarded them as habitual and
monstrous improprieties; the former as mere vagaries
of the moment, brought into play, certainly, without
forethought, but in perfect innocence and in want of
wrong motive. At home within his family circle, the
Ettrick Shepherd was a different being; he had the
feelings of the husband, the father, and the Christian
—and was, besides, without measure benevolent and
hospitable, full of those charities which commend
themselves to the heart, and so winning in his con-
duct and conversation as to subdue at once the stub-

born rebellions of prejudice, and remodel the preconceived notions of those who judged from surface
glimpses, and without any proper acquaintance.

I have often wondered at the respect paid to less
amiable men. How they are prated of and homaged
as patterns of moral worth—how their meagre virtues are bandied about from mouth to mouth, and
a dignity is given them greater than their merits—
how, because they industriously cloak up and conceal their foibles, therefore they are deemed ever
upright, without flaw or blemish, the embodied per-
sonifications of human propriety. Not, indeed, of
this sort was James Hogg!—he had none of the
solemn pragmatism of the scholastic grandee, none
of the starch and stiffness of the moral pedant. He
despised to affect a gravity and demureness foreign to
his buoyant and playful nature, and loved laughing
wisdom better than serious folly. I have an esteem
for his memory, which is injured none by the carpings
and prejudices of others. I knew the man better than
they did, and have ever regarded him as uniting in
his character many of the most valuable aspects of
human virtue.

But enough of this—James Hogg was a zealous
angler, and that is saying much for any man. He
had the mysteries of the craft at his finger-ends.
It was a part of his poetical existence to lavish the
forenoon hours abroad by the river-side, enticing the
yellow-fins with his big, brown hackles or scrutiniz-

ing the channels for a November fish, with a long, six-
pronged leister in his hands.    Latterly he patronized
the otter.    He was wrong, but his hands were perhaps
feebler, his dispositions less active than formerly, and
he hesitated to wade, as of old, along the margin of
St. Mary's Loch, when, without this fatigue, he might
continue the capture of some scores of half-pounders
and a kelt or two, lank, lean, large-headed, and
silvery.    The Shepherd was a persevering, and consequently a successful angler; but he never, in my
humble judgment, threw a nice fly; he was ignorant
of the proper sweep necessary to be taken before the
line could be fairly projected, and he had a strange
affection for strong coarse gut, and large heavy hooks,
superfluously loaded with feathers.    A flail might have
scanned the surface with more delicacy than his un-
trained tackle !    How he managed to catch fish at all,
was to me a marvel ; but they rose, not a doubt, to his
fly, and found an entrance also to his pannier.

Methinks I once more behold him wending his
way back to Altrive Cottage, clad in a grayish shoot-
ing-jacket of light summer fabric, with his pastoral
plaid, forming a cross in front, and knotted on the
left side, so as not to interfere with the use and exercise of his rod arm, over which waves one of Baillie
Grieve's best ties—worsted certainly, but still in
spring, and able to control the efforts of as noble
fish as ever swam upward from Yarrow fues.    Know
ye not the poet by his free, firm step ?—by the light

blue eye, reflecting nature in its joyous sphere?—by the forehead, solemn and lofty, in which the mind performs its mysteries, where the fragment of divinity in man upholds him in communion with his Maker? This is not a small creel pendant from his shoulders, and it is filled to the saugh-lid with clear, star-sided fish, elf-dolphins, a fairy gift from a kind water-sprite to our Shepherd-bard.

## A DAY'S ANGLING WITH THE ETTRICK SHEPHERD.

I dream! This is a past irrevocable vision—yet I remember it as of yesterday! Does it not seem like yesterday when we twain set forth from under the roof of Tibby Shiels, our hostess on St. Mary's Loch, to angle together far up among the hills in the burn of Winterhope? It was a half-drizzily, half-rainy morning, with a dash or two of wind at intervals, which considerably agitated the sheet of water, along whose margin, at outset, our road lay. Thick masses of mist floated across the heights, and the distant ravines, giving egress to a number of small torrents, mingled their continuous roar with the occasional gusts of the dying storm. An uncharitable sort of day it seemed for our angling excursion; but we had the expectation and trust that matters would mend, and so trudged on, in teeth of the weather.

After leaving the loch-side, our way led up a small glen, bisected by a black, mossy brook, on reaching the sources of which we conjectured ourselves at the summit of no inconsiderable hill. There, however, the mist was thick, rapid, and impenetrable, and a cold rain slanted athwart us, in large, ugly drops. Somewhat breathless with our upward ascent, we planted ourselves upon a tuft of thick heather, and, as the phrase goes, *took our morning* from the flask of mountain dew and its accompanying quaich—which, as a matter of course, we carried along with us. One plaid it was under which both of us, for the space of several minutes, were sheltered; but soon again we started along the level moss, with a strong, quick step, anxious to make the best of our time, and gain without delay the wished-for stream. But, wanting a compass, we had to struggle through a cursed obliterating fog; and although at the first instinctive of our course, we soon began to lose all knowledge of where we were. Track there was none among the chaos of moss-hags round about us. A solitary heath-cock whirred up in our van, and took its own path through the humid air, but we had no wings to follow the phantom bird; and the one-eyed pointer which accompanied us returned shivering to our feet, in marvel that the game had not dropped dead before her, out of sheer courtesy to her splendid abilities. And now a ragged sheep, seeming huge as a lion, started up at our side—it dived forward into the cloud, and vanished as if evaporated. But on we held, as our fancies directed us, having at whiles a dim, indistinct memory of some knoll or other—of this rude shepherd's cairn or of that heathery ridge—yet, no sooner recognisant of where we were, than again plunged into the circle of absolute ignorance.

Lost in a mist!—it was a pretty piece of knight-errantry! Through what a battalion of shadows had we to tilt our way! The wind blew in more directions than one, and even the mossy rills seemed to veer about and retrace their courses at our pursuit. Some of them became dead and stagnant, others escaped from our presence, we knew not where. Our converse was now monosyllabic and ejaculatory, but there was still a lightness at our hearts and in our step!—we were amused rather than distressed, for assured felt we, that human habitations were not out of reach, and that it was neither a Siberian desert nor Indian prairie within which we wandered.

The rain became at length more violent than ever, mingled with hail pellets, large and piercing.— What of that? a soaking was nothing extraordinary for anglers to encounter! We esteemed it no resignation to endure so petty an evil, and courted rather than shunned the boisterous elements. But lo! we were close by the margin of a sheet of water, and a hurra burst from both our lips, for well knew we Loch Skene—the dark, heath-fringed tarn.

LOCH SKENE.

What epicure could desire a richer, more delicate morsel, than a Loch Skene trout?—it is the
perfection of a fish—curves of a pink carnation
colour, and is creamed, betwixt the flakes, with a
white, oily, well-flavoured substance. Not large
is it, but thick-shaped, golden-hued, and firm, becoming after death ribbed over with irregular clouds on
a bright, dainty ground.

Our rods were soon up; we intended not to angle
there, but help it how could we, although Winterhope-burn was scarcely half a mile off? There
are few days that suit Loch Skene, and this was
not one of these. Its trout rise freest during a
warm, soft, south-west wind, in a small, quick ripple,
and a gentle rain; but the water at present was all
eddied and frothy, our lines were carried up from
its surface, and we were unable to guide to our
wishes the guileful fly. Not a dozen betwixt us in
two tedious hours did we capture; and, vexed at our
ill success, away again we set toward Winterhope-
burn; yet not till the mist had cleared off, and we
had sung out to the circle of hills, in order to stir
the slumber of an echo choir. Hymned back were
the rotund words, as if by a thousand voices, imitative
of misery—the misery of the damned!

WINTERHOPE-BURN.—MEGGAT-WATER.

It was a glorious day for stream-angling. The fountains of the hills were gushing over—every cavity was charged with water. How full and how finely coloured was Winterhope-burn!—All of its finny dwellers were astir! The first fall of our flies decided our fortune. We moved at half a mile's distance from each other. It would have been folly to have angled closer, especially along the upper part of the stream, which, although divided into fine promising pools, is still narrow and easily traversed. Lower down, it widens up considerably, and when meeting with Meggat-water, which it does after a run of two or three miles, offers, when in a swollen state, ample room for the closer exercise of two rods.

The weather had now greatly improved; there was a glimpse of blue sky over-head, and one of the hills at a distance was covered with sun-gleams. It was milder and calmer. The day's creation of flies was abroad—some of them skimming the air, and others, less secure, the margin of the pools. Nimbly and eagerly the trout rose, not in singleness but by pairs, darting at our deceitful hooks without caution or forethought. We hollo'd to each other on the capture of every fresh dozen, and frequently was our note of exultation repeated. The contents of our creels increased rapidly, and

ere four in the afternoon there was mustered betwixt
us above three stone weight! By this time, we had
angled over a considerable portion of Meggat-water,
and had reached, almost in company with each other,
the dark, deep pools lying immediately above the
Kirk. These, we well knew, contained a number of
prime and subtle fish—to be captured only when the
water, as at that time, was of a dark porter-colour.
Accordingly, we threw off our somewhat worn and
dismantled flies, exchanging them for others of a
larger and brighter sort, and, tossing for the choice
pool, commenced carefully to rake the water-surface.
Almost at the same moment, each of us happened
upon a sturdy two-pounder. They fought like heroes,
throwing themselves at full length out of the pool, and
pushing straight up against the current. Now they
relaxed a little, and showed their sides. They gasped
submission, and our bended wands brought them to
the margin. How lovely they looked, lying among
the pebbles, not as if in agony—they felt none—but
like a tribute-offering devoted to us, their conquerors;
and in our creels lovelier still, curled up over the rest of
their tribe, seemingly their monarchs or their patriarch
sires! These creels were full, crammed to the lid,
ere we arrived at the Henderland-rocks; but the
Shepherd had a game-bag, and I an honestly huge
couple of coat-pockets, so that we lacked betwixt us no
store-room!

St. Mary's Loch was again in view, but not as at

dawn, when we set forth, for now it was calm, beautiful, and serene. There were an handful or two of
clouds up amid the azure of heaven, indolently basking
in the retiring sun-rays. Spiritual existences were they
not, draperied with ether, curious of the evolutions of
spheres or the abodes of humanity ? At the meadow-
foot waded a heron, with his long skeleton-legs half
immersed in the ford ; but now, spreading his huge,
broad wings, away he sailed, homeward to his distant
nest. We were wet, tired, and hungry, willing to bid
our brief adieu to the river margin. Our tackle was
soon overhauled, and the contents of our creels emptied
out, side by side, upon the mossy sward.

I know not of a more generous feast for the eye
than a display of this nature ! It is worth a peep
at the regalia of an Eastern Khan. Here the very
confusion is the finest order. Were we to arrange the
fish in rows or pairs, according to their sizes, how stiff
and stall-like they would appear ; but tumble them
over carelessly upon the grass, and they will assume
attitudes of the greatest beauty. No ordinary take of
trout had we on that occasion ; in all, seven and
twenty dozen ; a couple of two and nine one-pounders,
fifty and more half the latter size, and the rest smaller
but not despicable fish.

Such was a memorable day's doings in company
with my late friend, the Ettrick Shepherd. Many
others have I spent of a similar sort, and none, can
I well recollect, which failed to exhibit feats on his

part of great prowess as an angler, although I take upon me to doubt that he displayed any degree of the science and system esteemed so highly by the Cockney school.

These sagacious rodsmen, armed with their cunning contrivances, equipped and tricked out in all manner of novelties, may, from sheer and intolerant conceit, turn up the fuming nostril at the plain and rustic enginery of the northern angler, with solemn eulogy exalting their unpractised theories, and making boastful exposure of their gleamy baubles;—yet, advance them to the proof, cause them to contest it with the artless craftsmen of Tweedside, and they will confess the utter impotence of their system, renouncing for unadorned simplicity the unnatural similitudes and grotesque inventions of the city artizan. The lure fascinates none the better because it is of brilliant texture or curious and expensive fabric, set off with orient plumage, and bedizened with ribs of tinsel;— more bewitching is the coarse and homely device fashioned after nature by the hands of the untaught peasant.

These remarks are perhaps over-strained, and entirely out of place. I make them out of a strong abhorrence to the practice of foppery, in an art which, by the good old rules of its patriarchs, ought to disclaim everything of the sort. An ape angling with humming-birds is too severe a caricature upon our craft, and we wish it to be rendered totally inapplicable.

To return to James Hogg.—He was in many particulars a good example of the old Border anglers. His notions concerning our rights were liberal in the extreme, and strong in their opposition to the narrow, selfish, and oppressive systems in force among northern aristocrats. He was persevering and enthusiastic, fond of adventure, and regardless of peril. He had a frank and generous disposition, warm feelings, and unequalled good-humour. With him there was no grumbling at the caprices of fortune, and he encountered her hardest rubs with singular indifference. Perhaps, indeed, this easy and immoveable temper of his was rather a failing than a virtue.

Happening to be at St. Mary's Loch, during the time of an event, by no means a happy one in the experience of Hogg, I was afforded an opportunity of judging with what calmness he encountered reverses of a distressful nature. It was at the period of his removal from Mount Benger to Altrive Lake— a circumstance attended, as his personal friends may recollect, with considerable grievances. Almost during the very progress of his removal, or but a day or two after, he walked up to the head of St. Mary's Loch with his rod in hand, and actually spent the night at Mrs. Richardson's cottage, nor was I able to discover the smallest abatement from his usual good spirits and cheerfulness. He conversed, laughed, and projected schemes of amusement, as if nothing had happened.

14

The Ettrick Shepherd owed much to his matri-
monial alliance. He had a sensible wife, and an affec-
tionate domestic circle. I shall ever regard his loss as
one of no common sort. It will destroy much of the
spirit of the Border land, wither many of its associations, and harm not a little the fine tone of fraternal
feeling which existed there. It will throw a melancholy
over the pastoral hills and the quiet valleys—over the
mouldering tower and the lowly cottage—across the
glassy lake and the shining river;—his imperishable song
will not fill up the place of its minstrel, nor supply
what is departed of the husband, the father, the friend,
the patriot, and the angler.

This lengthened oration of Tom Otter's seems to
have been listened to with beseeming attention by
the other members of the club, and was accordingly
followed up by their dedicating a toast to the
memory of the Forest-Poet. Topics, however, of
a less melancholy nature found, during the course
of the evening, their way into discussion, and the
right festive humour prevailed exceedingly. Our
recollections, we confess, in an attempt to methodize
and embody the principal matters touched upon on
the occasion of the fraternity's final meeting, have
proved disappointingly brittle; and we find ourselves under the necessity of merely subjoining a
few fragments of desultory discourse, along with

such angling verses as we have had the good fortune to keep in remembrance.

We may here mention, that the usage of the club in their festive meetings prohibited the introduction of all songs, save and except such as were strictly of a piscatory nature—and that by a special indulgence only, granted by the president, was it rendered allowable for the members present to launch out among staves and rondos of the more ordinary sorts. A law of this complexion was indeed requisite, in order to keep up the spirit of the fraternity; and only on rare occasions, when a certain period of the night had passed over, did the ruling member ever think it proper to lay it aside.

The following was sung by Harry Hackle, who, along with Tim Gaff, had joined the company shortly after Tom Otter had pronounced his lengthened eulogium on James Hogg. These gentlemen, it appears, popped in unexpectedly, on their return from a shooting excursion held at some distance from the club cottage. Three hares, a brace of old blackcock, and thirteen plump partridges, formed the produce of their day's sport—all of which were committed on arrival to the culinary hands of our worthy and discreet hostess.

[HACKLE *sings.*]

## Ye Warders of the Waters!

### I.

Ye warders of the waters !
Is the aldered stream-side free ?
  Hath the salmon sped
  From its winter bed
Adown to the azure sea ?
  Rideth afloat
  The fisher's boat
Below the white-thorn tree?

### II.

Go forth, ye anglers jovial !
The waters are open wide ;
  No longer we ward
  From vernal sward
The glittering salmon glide.
  Free at your will
  The crystal rill,
And tuneless torrent side.

### III.

Ho ! warders of the waters !
Is the yellow-trout at feed ?
  And the March-flies brown,
  Are they sailing down
Where current and zephyr lead ?
  See you abroad
  With pliant rod
Some gentle brother speed ?

IV.

Go forth, ye anglers jovial !
The ring of the trout we spy,
   And the south winds pour
   In a pleasant shower
The merry March-brown fly ;
   With vigorous wand
   The fisher hand
Among the dark pools ply.

*Swivel.* The day's labours, Harry, have in nowise lessened the vigour of thy song. But how is't thou preferrest the fowling-piece now-a-days, and puttest thy rod-arm out of practice ? 'Tis a leaning towards revolt in thee and Master Timothy, which I, Nathan Swiveltop, take upon me to reprehend.

*Hackle.* They are twin sports, Doctor, those of the stream and field——the one vernal, the other autumnal. ——Faith ! I love them both.

*Swivel.* Not without a preference, master renegade. Be honest, Harry, and detail to us thine angling exploits during the last three months.

*Hackle.* Ay ! that I will. Riddled with my gun three pike on the third of September ; marred a flying salmon on the nineteenth of August ; and, only a fortnight ago, pinked, off the coast of Ayrshire, an oily porpoise !

*Swivel.* Bravo ! Harry. And now, Tim, 'tis thy turn to give account of thyself——or, failing to do so, render a song instead.

[GAFF *sings.*]

## The Streams of Old Scotland for me!

### I.

The streams of Old Scotland for me !
   The joyous, the wilful, the wild ;
The waters of song and of glee,
That ramble away to the sea
   With the step and the mirth of a child !

### II.

The valleys of England are wide,
   Her rivers rejoice every one ;
In grace and in beauty they glide,
And water-flowers float at their side
   As they gleam in the rays of the sun.

### III.

But where is the speed and the spray ?
   The dark lakes that welter them forth ?
Tree and heath nodding over their way ?
The rock and the precipice grey,
   That bind the wild streams of the north ?

### IV.

Hath the salmon a dormient home
   In track of the barbel or bream ?
Or holds he his fastness of foam
Where the wraiths of the dark storm roam
   At the break of a wandering stream ?

v.

Even there you will find him, among
The glens of Old Scotland afar ;
And up through her valleys of song
He silently glances along,
In corslet of silver and star !

vi.

The rivers of Scotland for me !
They water the soil of my birth,
They gush from the hills of the free,
And sing, as they seek the wild sea,
With a hundred sweet voices of mirth !

*Otter.* And ever may they do so ! and ever may our craft continue to haunt them unrestricted ! May no rude, illiberal enactment, usurp from them the privilege bestowed by nature upon her lowliest children !

*Leister.* I fear, Tom, you supplicate in vain,—our rights, alas ! are daily abridged and interfered with. Streams, where one, a few years ago, might angle without challenge, are now shut out and protected ; and ere long our pastime will become fenced in with a set of arbitrary injunctions, compared with which the game laws themselves must appear clement and inoppressive !—But stiffen thy tumbler a degree, and favour us with a stave.

[OTTER *sings.*]

### Otter's Angling Song.

#### I.

Through sun-bright lakes,
  Round islets gay,
The river takes
  Its western way,
And the water-chime
Soft zephyrs time,
  Each gladsome summer day.

#### II.

The starry trout,
  Fair to behold,
Roameth about
  On fin of gold ;
At root of tree
His haunt you may see,
  Rude rock or crevice old.

#### III.

And hither dart
  The salmon grey,
From the deep heart
  Of some sea bay ;
And herling wild
Is here beguiled
  To hold autumnal play.

IV.

Oh ! 'tis a stream
  Most fair to see,
As in a dream
  Flows pleasantly,
And our hearts are woo'd
To a kind, sweet mood,
  By its wondrous witchery !

*May.* Here's a health to thee, Tom; yet, as for thy singing, I commend it not. To my judgment, thy cranium lacks the hill of tune.

*Otter.* I am glad on't, Master May-fly, seeing I shall thereby escape plague and persecution, the inevitable consequences of having the mood musical about one ;—but Swiveltop and you, it is alleged, are wont to practise duetts together by the stream-side, when the angling humour wears off, as it frequently does, betwixt you.—Marry ! let us have one.

*May.* That you shall, Tom—so join in, Doctor.

*Swivel.* Lead, Bill, lead, and trust to my assistance ; peradventure the words on't cross my memory.

[MAY-FLY *and* SWIVELTOP *sing.*]

𝕲𝖔𝖔𝖉 𝕮𝖍𝖊𝖊𝖗! 𝕭𝖗𝖔𝖙𝖍𝖊𝖗 𝕬𝖓𝖌𝖑𝖊𝖗, 𝖘𝖆𝖞.

MAY-FLY.

Good cheer ! brother angler, say,
Is the swift salmon abroad to-day ?
Have you noted the flash of his silvery mail,
Or the proud free curl of his glittering tail ?

Hath he sprung at the winsome fly,
  Smitten by the treacherous feather,
  Heedless of the steel and tether,
And of human subtlety ?


### SWIVELTOP.

Alas ! brother angler, nay,
Salmon none have I stirred to-day ;
Feint, frolic, nor dart, have I beheld ;
But round me the wily dark-trout belled—
One in greed, another in scorn,
  And a third one of pleasure
  Sprang at my fly—See, all the treasure
Ta'en by me this live-long morn !


### MAY-FLY.

Ply on, brother angler ! hark !
The grey wind warbles across the park ;
It ruffles the water from bank to bank,
And shakes the green covert of rushes lank.
See how it paces round and round,
  Wild of foot, with step unsteady,
  Dancing on the amorous eddy,
To a low, uncertain sound !


### BOTH.

Ply on, brother angler ! deep
Under the rapids the bright fins sweep,
And the salmon holdeth his secret track
O'er ledges of rock, through fissure black.
Oh ! most hath an angler need
  Of sweet patience and of plodding ;
  For the good wand, ever nodding,
Better than cunning, bringeth speed !

Due honours having been paid to Doctor Swivel-top and Mr. May-fly for this joint effusion, the latter gentleman thought it proper to fatigue the fraternity with a tedious, semi-political address—in the course of which, after acknowledging the complimentary civilities conferred on himself and his illustrious friend, he launched forth into a detail of his own wonderful feats as an angler, whereby it appeared that he had beaten hollow the powers of warlockry in unfolding the secrets of certain lochs and rivers, the finny inhabitants of which had, without doubt, established a subterraneous communication with the great lakes of North America, such was their power, speed, voracity, and amplitude. Previous, however, to the delivery of this rhapsodical oration by the somewhat elevated member, our friend Jack Leister volunteered the following song :—

[LEISTER *sings*.]

The breeze is on the Heron-lake!

I.

The breeze is on the Heron-lake !
  The May-sun shineth clear !
Away we bound through the broomy brake,
  With our wands and angling gear.

II.

The birch-wreath o'er the water-edge
  Scatters sweet flies about,
And round his haunt of sighing sedge
  Bells up the yellow trout.

### III.

Beware ! beware ! his eye is bright
  As falcon's in the sky :
But artful feather, hove aright,
  Will hood a keener eye.

### IV.

Beware ! beware ! the water-weed
  And the birch that waves behind,
And gently let the good line speed
  Before thee on the wind.

### V.

O gently let the good line flow,
  And gently wile it home ;
There's many a gallant fin, I trow,
  Under the ribbed foam.

### VI.

A merry fish on a stallion hair,
  'Tis a pleasant thing to lead,
On May-days, when the cowslip fair
  Is blooming on the mead ;

### VII.

When the breeze is up, and the sun is out,
  And grey flies two or three
Sport in the noon-tide, round about
  The shadow of a tree.

### VIII.

O then the heart bounds pleasantly,
  And its thoughts are pleasant things,
Gushing in joyous purity,
  Like silent water-springs !

Of Mr. May-fly's address, by which the above was succeeded, we forbear offering more than a single extract, relative to a certain angling feat vaunted of by him—for the truth of which, however, we hold ourselves in nowise responsible. An exploit, similar in some points, was once narrated to us by a gentleman whose veracity we had every reason to rely on, and singular to say, the same locality was assigned to it which is spoken of by our worthy brother, as having formed the scene of the following adventure.

### MAY-FLY'S PERILOUS ANGLING FEAT.

" I trust, gentlemen," continued he, after much previous detail, " I trust to your further forbearance for permission to recount another of those singular angling feats which it was my good fortune lately to perform. You are most of you acquainted with the stream connecting Loch Lydoch with Lochs Aich and Rannoch, and are aware that it contains, among innumerable quantities of small trout, some of a very superior description. While fly-fishing there last summer, and in the act of tossing out a pair of puny individuals, I was surprised by a singular agitation of the water behind them, which was repeated again after a few seconds, farther up the pool. Conceiving this double movement to be occasioned by a large fish in pursuit of food, I immediately substituted for the slender tackle I had hitherto employed, an ordinary pike-hook, with its wire arming, affixing thereto one of the small fry just captured.

" Proceeding, thus equipped, a few yards up the stream, I allowed my bait to drop gently into the centre of a strong, dark-coloured eddy, within which it was no sooner enveloped, than I became sensible of its being seized by a pair of powerful jaws. Immediately also, a steady determination thereof towards the opposite bank warned me to give out line with my hand from the reel. On finding this, however, speedily exhausted by the determined progress of the fish across the stream, I thought it proper to strike sharply; and no sooner, gentlemen, was this accomplished, than there came at once to view the fluke of a prodigious tail, announcing to me the presence of a fish at least five stone in weight ! (*Great cheering.*)

" I do not exaggerate—I am incapable of exaggerating. Five stone ! be it repeated, was the weight of this fish ; and the sequel, gentlemen, should you listen to me, will remove all doubts of my veracity.

" Before I could well recover from the astonishment caused in me by the partial display of such a monster, he commenced ascending the river at an able pace, but by no means so rapidly as to occasion his pursuer over-much distress. In fact, to my best recollection, I was not constrained to yield above four fathoms of line during the whole run, which lasted fifteen minutes at a moderate calculation, and took me a mile's distance from the spot where I first encountered him. When at length the fish halted, which he did with singular suddenness, and more seemingly by way of whim than from fatigue, I began to make calculations as to the possibility of securing him before night, seeing that the afternoon was already far advanced, and my situation in the uninhabited and swampy moor, should darkness happen to overtake me, was not to be regarded as one altogether free from peril.

"Being, however, unwilling to break from the chance I possessed of capturing a trout so enormous, I found it necessary to put in practice some means, in order to rouse him as quickly as possible from the lethargic and immoveable position assumed by him after his recent exertions; as, without doing so, I had no likelihood of so fatiguing the fish as to obtain a speedy conquest over him. Accordingly, I committed myself with great caution to the water—which, be it remarked, was deep, rapid, and, as to the footing it afforded, not a little precarious. Scarcely, indeed, had I advanced three paces, before I found myself engulphed waist-high, and on the point of being carried downward by the strength of the current!

"At this moment, however, a sudden strain on my line indicated the intentions of the fish to renew his run; whereupon, more regardful of him than of my own peril, I only clenched my rod with the greater vigour, and relying on the strength of tackle with which I happened to be provided, actually suffered myself to be dragged forward into the midst of a black, dangerous pool !—Here, fortunately, through the assistance of my left arm, I kept pretty fairly afloat, and managed at the same time to control a desperate plunge of the infuriated fish, who forthwith, finding all such exertion to no purpose, resumed his career up the river.

" Gentlemen, I cannot describe to you my situation at this juncture. I have no recollection of how I felt and acted for the space of some minutes, seeing that such must have elapsed before I again found myself able rationally to decide what steps, consistent with the honour of an angler, it were best for me to pursue. I had been hauled upwards of an hundred yards through the centre of the water, and was now lying, altogether exhausted, on a shoal-bed of gravel. My rod, strange to say, remained uninjured in my grasp, and instinctively I felt apprised of the continued presence of the great fish, again at rest, within the distance of five paces. He had, however, fortunately, no inclination to stir fin previous to my reaching *terra firma*, on the south bank of the river, where, by the aid of my flask, I was enabled ere long to regain a good portion of my lost strength and courage ; which having done, I commenced a violent attack with sods and stones upon the spot where he lay, and speedily had the gratification of beholding him at full sail down the stream. Following, of course, as fast as the drenched state of my habiliments allowed me, I felt further encouraged by an indication of great exhaustion on the part of the fish, who evidently had lost the power of retaining his proper balance, and not unfrequently rolled over, belly-uppermost, in the water. This, however, might have been a stratagem of his to put me off my guard, as all of a sudden he sprang directly into the air, and would certainly have shivered my tackle, had I not become instinctively aware of the movement, and provided for it forthwith, by lowering the point of the rod. Finding himself thus baffled, the fish seemed in no humour to resume his descent, but commenced thrusting with his snout against the opposite marge of the river, from which, however, hastily recoiling, he took a cross run towards that on which I stood, and continued without intermission, for nearly a quarter of an hour, passing and repassing betwixt the two banks.

It was now growing dark—I was far from any dwelling, and possessed of a very imperfect knowledge of the wide and dangerous moor with which I was surrounded ; moreover, I had the hunger of a wolf, and was thoroughly soaked to boot ;—yet, gentlemen, for the honour of our craft, I resolved to remain and subject to the dominion of the wand a fish, I feel assured, without its equal in broad Scotland. Nor was I long in so doing, and that in the manner which I shall now relate to you.

The part of the river which I had at this time reached happened to branch off in two separate streams, which, joining again below, formed a small

15

island. Through the principal of these I had already been conducted by the fish during his ascent, and it was now my fortune, being on the opposite side of the water from where I then was, to direct him in a manner along the other, which, although in some parts nearly as broad, was by no means either so deep or rapid as the main branch. In fact, at a short distance above their reunion it was crossed by a bar of gravel, which had the effect, while it widened, of greatly obstructing and shallowing off the stream.

Upon this, the fish, in an attempt to carry himself clean over it, fortunately ran aground, and owing to his fatigued state, and the great bulk he possessed, proved unable to force his way back again into deep water. I immediately marched forward through the stream, recovering line on my way, until I came into close contact with him, and found the monster jammed in as it were betwixt two furrows of gravel, which, by means of his chin, he had reared up on either side of him. Instantly pulling out a large pocket-knife—the same, gentlemen, which I now exhibit to you—I rushed upon my prize, inflicting across his spine the fatal gash! It was, to the best of my recollection, as it were, done upon the mane of an earthquake, so violent and terrible was the death of this water-lord! Blood, sand, and pebbles, were flung about on all sides of me, and I narrowly escaped being laid prostrate by a tail-blow from the infuriated fish! After the lapse, however, of a few seconds, life became extinct, and I dragged him exultingly to the water-edge, there to quaff off to his memory the remainder of my flask, and devise in what manner to bear home-wards, through moor and darkness, a trophy so magni-ficent.

My first idea was to conceal the fish in some hollow or other, and endeavour to thread my way towards the inn, which lay several miles off in the neighbourhood of Loch Rannoch, whence, on the day following, I should set out to fetch him, having procured proper assistance. I regret, indeed, that this plan was not pursued, as, had it been, I should probably have escaped the mortification I was destined to suffer, in being obligated to relinquish so noble a prize. Un-willing, however, to proceed without him, I took it into my head, as a good expedient, that I might readily, by means of my tackle, which remained as yet unextricated from his gorge, float the fish forward down the Gawin and through Loch Aich to within a few yards of where I intended to quarter for the night.

Accordingly, I commenced the attempt, but had scarcely proceeded above two hundred paces, when my attention was directed to the plunge of a large animal immediately below me, and before I could drag in my captive out of harm's way, he was in the grasp of a powerful otter! In vain, gentlemen, did I shout; in vain rush forward into the stream; tackle and fish both had disappeared in a twinkling;—the rascal had carried all away with him. To say more, would be

to describe the feelings of one crazed by misfortune !
I know not to this day how I reached Loch Rannoch——

*Swivel.* On the back of a hippopotamus, was it not,
Bill ?—Say so, man, an thou wantest credit for this
exploit of thine ! To superadd a marvel or twain
will improve the effect on't, and in nowise harm its
probability !

*May.* Courtesy, it appears, Nathan, is no director
of thy faith.

*Swivel.* If so, Bill, my creed would be a monstrous one.

*May.* Marry, indeed ! Doctor—thou hast swallowed rawer fictions ere now than are of my fashion-
ing. How little credit findeth an angler's tale !
'Tis among truths unsworn to, the oftest ridiculed.
Men stare on't, as it were moon-dropt, and would
take the say of a pagan into more account.

*Swivel.* Well might they, Master May-fly, opining
from these feats of thine.—But how, gentlemen, is
the bowl ran dry ?

[*Sings.*]

### Farewell to the Season.

I.

We part not thus !—nay, anglers, nay—
    A farewell to the season !
So fill the bowl and drink away,
    Who drinks not harbours treason.

II.

O fill it high ! the joyous draught
   Is native to our heather ;
If bravely drained and largely quaffed,
   'Twill bind our hearts together.

III.

Now wintry winds, with rapid pace,
   O'er mead and mountain sally ;
And gloomily the waters race
   Through each deserted valley

IV.

No more sweet birds, in merry strain,
   Sing from their bowers of beauty ;
Lay down the wand—the spring again
   Will call it forth for duty.

V.

Lay down the wand—no longer now
   The fearful trout is belling ;
All leafless left, the alder bough
   Moans o'er his glassy dwelling.

VI.

Then heap, heap high our social hearth !
   Why should the good fire flicker ?
And quaff ! quaff on !—The best of mirth
   Lies deepest in the liquor !

*May.* And best of melody to boot, Doctor; thou art tun'd to the point of admiration. But these are voices familiar to us outside ?—Hark you ?

*Leister.* So methinks, Bill, albeit when or where heard, I recollect not.

*Otter.* Marry do I; an it be not Mark Wandle-weir and Master Herl-broke, Tom Otter is other than Tom Otter.

*Leister.* Thou sayest it. Welcome, gentlemen, most welcome. [*Enter* WANDLE-WEIR *and* HERL-BROKE.] Hilloa ! mistress, loads of comfort ; bring fire, water, meats and marrows—with cordials cunning and strengthy—hose and hot slippers ; there be two here who have dropt out of a cloud, blastworn and wetted throat high.

*Wandle.* A pitiable account of us, Mr. Leister ; but in truth thou hast hit the mark. How fares it with our loving fraternity ?

*Swivel.* Right bountifully, gentle brother,· This, you may note, is our feast of farewells, whereat we encase our wands, close our panniers, and determine our retreat from the stream-side. But play thy part at the tren-cher, good sir ; thou must unfold a tale of thy wander-ings ere we separate.

*Wandle.* Willingly, Doctor. You shall have the arcana of my exploits at a beck, although, to speak the truth, I have proved an adventureless adventurer.

*Swivel.* And hast achieved nothing worthy of thy craft ?

*Wandle.* Nay, I said not so : never was hand more gory. But a truce, a truce, sweet Doctor good, let forks wag before tongues.

*Swivel.* Amen ! valiant sir.

[After partaking of the bountiful repast provided by our worthy landlady, Messrs. Wandle-weir and Herl-broke proceeded to amuse the club with an account of their wanderings in the north. It is not, however, within the province of these pages to enter into any elaborate detail of the manifold incidents met with by our intelligent brethren of the angle; we find it incumbent to offer nothing further than such portions of their relation as have reference to the pastime daily pursued by them among the least frequented of our Highland lochs and rivers. To this purpose we shall devote the following chapter.]

# CHAPTER XIV.

## THE ACHIEVEMENTS OF WANDLE-WEIR AND HERL-BROKE.

I TAKE it for granted, gentlemen (commenced Mr. Wandle-weir as spokesman on the occasion), that you are already made acquainted with the result of our rod operations up to the end of July last. My friend Herl-broke, if I remember rightly, addressed a communication to your honourable club, under the intention of regaling his brother members with a spice of our doings and sufferings on certain angling stations, north of the Tay. Our chief matters of complaint, should you recollect, were the dryness of the season, want of winds, and the incessant torment we met with from hordes of gad-flies, which haunted our steps with provoking pertinacity along the water's-edge. From a combination of maladies so unlooked for, it was natural for us to determine our escape. Measures accordingly were taken for a retreat homewards, and our journey had actually commenced, when down pops one of the loveliest showers imaginable—a glorious, soul-stirring, nerve-renewing thunder-plump! Never was one resolve so thoroughly dissipated for another by this unexpected discharge of the element. We had been waiting at Fort-William the arrival of one of the steamers plying betwixt Inverness and Glasgow, with the intention of joining her on her voyage south, when the first wild peal burst down from Nevis, gathering in the responses of a thousand lesser hills, recognizant all of their chieftain's terrific slogan.

*May.* Quite poetical grown, Mr. Wandle-weir; thou hast stocked a note-book with rhymes and images, I venture to infer.

*Wandle.* Nay, my humour was not so inclined. But to proceed. Allowing the smoky conveyance (a glimpse of whose tall funnel, walking the great canal into Loch Eil, we had been so anxious for two long days to obtain, and which, just as the last shower-drop reached the earth, glided triumphantly into view), allowing, I say, the murky water-coach to wheel onward, out we danced, Herl-broke and myself (our friend Smoulter-jaws having waved his adieus some days previous), toward Lochy-side, where, at the distance of a stone's-throw above the castle, we lit upon some shoals of princely sea-trout, fresh from the brine. Of these, we took no less than thirteen out of a single pool—the largest weighing upwards of four pounds, and as fleet, wary, and nimble a fish, as ever line thwarted. But our good

fortune was not destined to cease here, and we had
soon the further gratification of showing the rod-butt
to three prime grilses and one salmon, which latter
was anchored on by myself in midst of a perilous
eddy, out of which I found it no easy task to force
him, and prevent the cutting of my line on certain
sharp-toothed rocks which lay in the direction he aimed
at.    Luckily, however, my tackle was not deficient in
strength, and on putting it resolutely to the test,
I was able to effect the wished for control over my
fish, and ere long to gaff and secure him.    I will not,
however, detain you with any further mention of our
angling exploits in this quarter.    Zealous craftsmen as
we were, our appetite for sport became strangely im-
paired by the want of those scenic attractions, which
operate like sunshine on the heart, and keep the
springs of joy open within it.    The savage desolate-
ness of the surrounding moorland had greatly lowered
our spirits, and we shrunk away after a week's residence at Fort-William, like guilty things that had
busied ourselves with butcheries, not of fish, but of
our fellows.

The next scene of our achievements (continued
Mr. Wandle-weir) was Loch Ness.    Hiring a boat
early on the morning after our arrival at Fort-
Augustus, we beat up and down both sides of this
beautiful expanse of water, without so much as
stirring a single fin until the approach of noon,

when the breeze stiffening, we were fortunate enough to capture several good-sized trout and a brace of noble salmon. Here we were shown a fish weighing fourteen pounds, of the ordinary loch variety, which had been taken during the previous day by means of a spinning bait. It was reckoned a fair pattern of build in a trout of its dimensions, but did not strike me as nearly so magnificent a fish as the *salmo ferox* of Loch Awe, of which your club, gentlemen, possesses such an admirable specimen. I have caught trout from our English waters, which struck me as infinitely more attractive in form, and not a whit inferior to it in complexion.

*May.* To my mind, bulk is the prime matter, Master Wandle-weir. I account the beauty of a fish as nothing, provided it weigh like a mill-stone.

*Swivel.* Betake thee to the Arctics, Bill, and "bob for whales."

*May.* Not yet, Doctor, not yet—I am in nowise weary of thy company. But pardon our interruption.

*Wandle.* It would be tiresome, gentlemen, to all parties were I to detail circumstantially the numerous excursions Mr. Herl-broke and myself engaged in during our stay at Fort-Augustus. The Garry, Morriston, Oich, Foyers, Coiltie, and Enneric, were all visited in succession, nor did we neglect running a fly over two or three of the best reputed lochs, situated in the surrounding district of country.

Fish, of course, were not always on the fin, and we
had, upon more than one occasion, to hold ourselves
satisfied with an empty pannier.    The grandeur of the
scenes, however, among which our wanderings introduced us, amply compensated for the want of success
occasionally encountered.

[Here Mr. Wandle-weir digressed into an eulogium on
various natural beauties discovered to him during the
course of the above excursions, after which he amused
the club with an account of the piscatory raid under-
taken by him and his friend Herl-broke into Ross-shire.
We have no design, however, of following our worthy
brother-anglers along this portion of their tour, having
already, in a previous chapter, entered somewhat at
large into an analysis of the various waters belonging
to the several districts which they visited.    We shall
only confine our observations, in regard to the country
alluded to, within the limits of a single interrogatory,
addressed by our intelligent narrator to the members
of the club.    The purport of Mr. Wandle-weir's inquiry
was as to the reasonableness of a statement he had
seen repeatedly advanced among northern journalists,
whereby it was made to appear that an alarming decrease
had of late years taken place in the quantity both of
salmon and trout frequenting such streams as discharge
themselves along the Western coasts of Scotland, and,
moreover, that this decrease was owing solely to the recent
introduction of sheep into those pasture-grounds which
border on the waters in question.]

*May.*  What ! Mr. Wandle-weir, sheep devour salmon !
They say, 'tis true, goats will bolt vipers.

*Swivel.* And pigs eat bairns! Bill.

*Wandle.* I believe, gentlemen, no such unnatural propensity is intended to be attributed to the pecoral tribe. The destruction chiefly complained of is imagined to be in operation against the ova and fry of the fish. Wool-washing — the abridgment of food presumed to have taken place on the substitution of sheep for black cattle (which, as you all know, formerly constituted the live stock of the districts to which I allude)—and numerous other causes, are brought forward in support of this singular allegation.

*Leister.* Singular, Mr. Wandle-weir, you may well call it. It is, besides, utterly irrational, and at variance with what happens to be observed in the Southern districts of Scotland. Of a piece, notwithstanding, it seems with other attempts made by the prejudiced Highlanders to resist the introduction of sheep into our Northern pasturegrounds. I need only, however, in order to prove its inconsistency with fact, direct your attention to what happens to be the case in Selkirkshire—a county where it will be allowed the woolly tribe is reared to no inconsiderable extent. You are yourself acquainted with many of its numerous streams, such especially as have their channel and origin among sheep-pastures, and cannot fail to agree with me, that of these, one and all are crowded with trout almost beyond belief, and that during the autumnal and hibernal months they are visited, although lying at a great distance from the sea, by salmon and other fish, not singly or at infrequent intervals, but in large and continued masses.

*Otter.* You say truly, Jack. I have seen no less than forty or fifty gallant fins abstracted by a party of black-fishers from one pool, and that the very one into which the neighbouring sheep-farmers were accustomed to drive their flocks during the washing-month !

*Wandle.* It is, however, to be confessed, Mr. Otter, that the purifying operations performed upon the wool of sheep do in some measure affect the salubrity of those waters wherein they are carried on.

*Otter.* This I do not deny. The impregnating of a burn or pool with the corrupt smearing materials attached, among other filth, to the fleece, before clipping, cannot fail for the moment to sicken and alarm the delicate inhabitants of the stream. No serious result, however, takes place ; as far, at any rate, as my experience goes, I do not remember to have stumbled upon a single fish, small or great, in which the vital spark had been rendered extinct, owing to the cause above alleged.

[Some further conversation here took place among the
members of the club relative to the decrease of game
in pastoral districts.    This discussion, however, we
are urged to pass over, with a view of conducting our
readers along with Messrs. Wandle-weir and Herl-
broke, after their departure from Ross-shire.    Their
success among the streams and lakes of that county
was fully as great as they had anticipated, although
the weather encountered by them was not of the description which the angler reckons most favourable.
About the commencement of September, and a fortnight
previous to the time when the waters north of the Tweed
are closed up, we discover our lately installed brethren of
the wand among the mountainous regions of Strath-Glass,
descending which, they shortly afterwards reach Inverness, and strike onward from thence into Morayshire.
We must, however, give the conclusion of their angling
adventures in Mr. Wandle-weir's own words.]

We had now arrived (continued he) at the Findhorn, where it passes under the bridge of Dulsie.
Much as I have witnessed of river scenery, my
recollections are unable to call up any continued
stretch of bold decorations, equal to what is possessed by this noble stream.    From the Streens to
the Suspension-bridge near Forres, a distance, following its course, of not less than fifteen miles, one
unbroken chain of magnificent landscape is presented.
With a body of water sufficiently large to attract
attention, the Findhorn makes its way betwixt masses
of rock, imposing, equally from their height, their
form, and their distribution.    Trees, the skirts of a
forest, old and fantastic, peer over its parapets

mingled with shrubs and saplings, which steal down luxuriantly among the rill-worn fissures. Here, with imprecating arms, a storm-cleft oak towers over the abyss — there an ivy mourns — and, beyond it,

> " Self-pleased, a graceful birch
> Nods to its image in the glassy pool."

To eye Findhorn to advantage, one must adopt the angler's method of river-coursing. Its channel he must convert into his highway, and plunge unhesitatingly through such fords as promise to lead him towards the best view-stances and juts of observe. Your knapsack-tourists will gain nothing by confining themselves to the pinnacles and embankments; they must e'en descend to the water's surface, and look for an eye-feast upwards, not, as is their use, over and across.

As an angling water, we found Findhorn at certain points incomparable. The period, however, of our visit was such that it required little or no skill to take fish. Five, eleven, and nine salmon, were the several results of our operations during the three days preceding the 15th, when the waters, to our great disappointment, became shut up, and we were forced to adopt our route southward, without testing, as we originally intended, the primest of salmon-rivers, Spey.

*May.* A mighty mortification, indeed, Master

Wandle-weir, after the havoc committed by you and Herl-broke ! 'Twere time, methinks, to put the pannier aside with good will, instead of lusting afresh, against law and reason.

*Swivel.* The soul of an angler hath gone out of thee, Bill.

*May.* Not so, but its cravings, Doctor, are time-subdued. I despise to be affected by the throbs and longings of a school-boy heart, such as were wont of old to accompany me, while trudging forth, during play hours, to hitch out minnows from a water tank.

*Swivel.* Then are you grown a philosopher, Bill. 'Tis a change for the worse, an it be true. We must have no stoics among us, Master May-fly.

*May.* A sapient resolution. Lead down the aqua, Doctor. What, Tim, anchored already ?—and thou, Master Hackle ? Replenish, I pray you, my merry men all.

*Otter.* Keep the concord, Bill, lest we bind and bed thee. Free and good-humoured, without break or brawl, should be our Feast of Farewells. No apple of contention ought ever to lie upon its board. It should be a sealing up of the friendships of the year, that they may be kept faithful until we meet again. But, gentlemen——  ,

16

And further than this we can add nothing.—Of what Mr. Otter observed in continuation, we are left totally in the dark. Reader ! go on for the moral to our conclusion. Say we not, with Solomon—

" All things are vanity."

## CONCLUSION.

OUR matter is at an end. We possess no other relics of our loved fraternity—and what, gentle angler, are these before thee, save an unassorted, imperfect medley? We have not troubled ourselves to trick them out for favour. They are better, perhaps, as they are, even with all their likeness to those lettered follies which the day gives birth to.

.    .         .    .    .

.              .    .    .

Will the angling fraternity at C—— ever revive? Alas! the conclusion that our hearts come to is, that it never will. We have reason to believe that its dissolution has been a final one! There are no signs or chances of returning animation among us. The electric fires of sympathy are all gone out. Even

the tenement where our festive meetings were wont
to be held begins to show symptons of disrepair.    Its
kirtle gay of briars and woodbines now hangs about it
in careless shreds—the thatch has been partly torn
away, while what remains thereof is furred over with
wind-sown mosses ;—there is a huge fissure from base
to chimney-top at one end of the building, and several
great stones are commencing their escape outward
above the porch.    Its diamond-shaped panes, moreover, are many of them supplanted by patches of
vellum—abstractions, probably, from some ancient
manuscript formerly possessed by our club, and left,
unthought of, to the spoiler's mutilating hand.

Ah ! and our hostess too—our mirth-loving, kind-
hearted landlady, is no longer to be seen.    A stranger
fills. her place.    The tones of sweet humour and
benevolence which circled below her hospitable roof
are exchanged for the austere brawlings of a drunken
publican.    There is a sign-board also, swinging aloof
over the door-way, with the likeness of a fish pictured
upon it—surely not that of a salmon—a creature set
and proportioned so singularly never cleft the flood ;—
it seems a compound of the tench and the tad-pole,
and is coloured over with a sloughy, blue mixture, such
as might be formed from the cleanings of some well-

daubed palette. At one end of this murky monster is represented a big-bellied bottle, with its accompanying gill-stoup; at the other depends the figure of a huge fly-hook or parrot pad; while immediately over these, along the top of the board, one may discern, painted in big, black characters, "THE FISHER'S TRYST."

The Fisher's Tryst! Pity the angler that ventures below its ungracious rafters! In vain will he look for the rural pleasaunces they so lately overshadowed. Its once tidy furniture is mostly removed, while a couple of deal benches, guarding on either side a coarse, oaken table, occupy instead the principal apartment. The recess beds have both been robbed of their pannellings, and lie exposed in offensive disorder towards the entrance. One chair, halt and maimed, leans its fractured form against the narrow portion of wall by which these are divided, and a mirror (we recognise it as an ancient friend) is suspended directly over its back. Nothing happy may ever look again upon that darkening surface!

> " They cannot smile on't,
> Who trim their count'nance at its perilous front."

We turn with a shiver from this reflector of the human face divine—the loved things we looked for are there no longer !    We turn with a shiver from the now desecrated dwelling, and its sordid inmates,—from the stream, too—and why from *it ?*

> " Still its waters glide,
>     Unsullied at our side,
>     Making sweet music through the valley wide."

Why, then, turn from *it ?*—where the change that urges us to this ?—It lies, gentle angler, within our own heart !

THE  END.

PRINTED BY ROBERT MACLEHOSE, UNIVERSITY PRESS, GLASGOW.

# NEW BOOKS AND NEW EDITIONS.

*THE WOLFE OF BADENOCH.* A Historical Romance of the Fourteenth Century. By SIR THOMAS DICK LAUDER. Complete unabridged edition. Thick Crown 8vo. Price 6s.

*This most interesting romance has been frequently described as equal in interest to any of Sir Walter Scott's historical tales. This is a complete unabridged edition, and is uniform with " Highland Legends " and " Tales of the Highlands," by the same author. As several abridged editions of the work have been published, especial attention is drawn to the fact that the above edition is complete.*

*THE LIVES OF THE PLAYERS.* By JOHN GALT, Esq. Post 8vo. Price 5s.

*Interesting accounts of the lives of distinguished actors, such as Betterton, Cibber, Farquhar, Garrick, Foote, Macklin, Murphy, Kemble, Siddons, &c., &c. After the style of Johnson's " Lives of the Poets."*

*KAY'S EDINBURGH PORTRAITS.* A Series of Anecdotal Biographies, chiefly of Scotchmen. Mostly written by JAMES PATERSON. And edited by JAMES MAIDMENT, Esq. Popular Edition. 2 Vols., Post 8vo. Price 12s.

*A popular edition of this famous work, which, from its exceedingly high price, has hitherto been out of the reach of the general public. This edition contains all the reading matter that is of general interest; it also contains eighty illustrations.*

*THE RELIGIOUS ANECDOTES OF SCOTLAND.* Edited by WILLIAM ADAMSON, D.D. Thick Post 8vo. Price 5s.

*A voluminous collection of purely religious anecdotes relating to Scotland and Scotchmen, and illustrative of the more serious side of the life of the people. The anecdotes are chiefly in connection with distinguished Scottish clergymen and laymen, such as Rutherford, Macleod, Guthrie, Shirra, Leighton, the Erskines, Knox, Beattie, M'Crie, Eadie, Brown, Irving, Chalmers, Lawson, Milne, M'Cheyne, &c., &c. The anecdotes are serious and religious purely, and not at all of the ordinary witty description.*

*DAYS OF DEER STALKING* in the Scottish Highlands, including an account of the Nature and Habits of the Red Deer, a description of the Scottish Forests, and Historical Notes on the earlier Field Sports of Scotland. With Highland Legends, Superstitions, Folk-Lore, and Tales of Poachers and Freebooters. By WILLIAM SCROPE. Illustrated by Sir Edwin and Charles Landseer. Demy 8vo. Price 12s. 6d.

"*The best book of sporting adventures with which we are acquainted.*"—ATHENÆUM.

"*Of this noble diversion we owe the first satisfactory description to the pen of an English gentleman of high birth and extensive fortune, whose many amiable and elegant personal qualities have been commemorated in the diary of Sir Walter Scott.*"—LONDON QUARTERLY REVIEW.

*DAYS AND NIGHTS OF SALMON FISHING* in the River Tweed. By WILLIAM SCROPE. Illustrated by Sir David Wilkie, Sir Edwin Landseer, Charles Landseer, William Simson, and Edward Cooke. Demy 8vo. Price 12s. 6d.

"*Mr. Scrope's book has done for salmon fishing what its predecessor performed for deer stalking.*"—LONDON QUARTERLY REVIEW.

"*Mr. Scrope conveys to us in an agreeable and lively manner the results of his more than twenty years' experience in our great Border river. . . . The work is enlivened by the narration of numerous angling adventures, which bring out with force and spirit the essential character of the sport in question. . . . Mr. Scrope is a skilful author as well as an experienced angler. It does not fall to the lot of all men to handle with equal dexterity, the brush, the pen, and the rod, to say nothing of the rifle, still less of the leister under cloud of night.*"—BLACKWOOD'S MAGAZINE.

*THE FIELD SPORTS OF THE NORTH OF EUROPE.* A Narrative of Angling, Hunting, and Shooting in Sweden and Norway. By CAPTAIN L. LLOYD. New edition. Enlarged and revised. Demy 8vo. Price 9s.

"*The chase seems for years to have been his ruling passion, and to have made him a perfect model of perpetual motion. We admire Mr. Lloyd. He is a sportsman far above the common run.*"—BLACKWOOD'S MAGAZINE.

"*This is a very entertaining work and written, moreover, in an agreeable and modest spirit. We strongly recommend it as containing much instruction and more amusement.*—ATHENÆUM.

*PUBLIC AND PRIVATE LIBRARIES OF GLAS-GOW.* A Bibliographical Study. By THOMAS MASON. Demy 8vo. Price 12s. 6d. net.

*A strictly Bibliographical work dealing with the subject of rare and interesting works, and in that respect describing three of the public and thirteen of the private libraries of Glasgow. All of especial interest.*

*THE LIFE OF SIR WILLIAM WALLACE.* By JOHN D. CARRICK. Fourth and cheaper edition. Royal 8vo. Price 2s. 6d.

*The best life of the great Scottish hero. Contains much valuable and interesting matter regarding the history of that historically important period.*

*THE HISTORY OF THE PROVINCE OF MORAY.* By LACHLAN SHAW. New and Enlarged Edition, 3 Vols., Demy 8vo. Price 30s.

*The Standard History of the old geographical division termed the Province of Moray, comprising the Counties of Elgin and Nairn, the greater part of the County of Inverness, and a portion of the County of Banff. Cosmo Innes pronounced this to be the best local history of any part of Scotland.*

*HIGHLAND LEGENDS.* By SIR THOMAS DICK LAUDER. Crown 8vo. Price 6s.

*Historical Legends descriptive of Clan and Highland Life and Incident in former times.*

*TALES OF THE HIGHLANDS.* By SIR THOMAS DICK LAUDER. Crown 8vo. Price 6s.

*Uniform with and similar in character to the preceding, though entirely different tales. The two are companion volumes.*

*AN ACCOUNT OF THE GREAT MORAY FLOODS IN 1829.* By SIR THOMAS DICK LAUDER. Demy 8vo., with 64 Plates and Portrait. Fourth Edition. Price 8s. 6d.

*A most interesting work, containing numerous etchings by the Author. In addition to the main feature of the book, it contains much historical and legendary matter relating to the districts through which the River Spey runs.*

*OLD SCOTTISH CUSTOMS:* Local and General. By E. J. GUTHRIE. Crown 8vo. Price 3s. 6d.

*Gives an interesting account of old local and general Scottish customs, now rapidly being lost sight of.*

---

*A HISTORICAL ACCOUNT OF THE BELIEF IN WITCHCRAFT IN SCOTLAND.* By CHARLES KIRKPATRICK SHARPE. Crown 8vo. Price 4s. 6d.

*Gives a chronological account of Witchcraft incidents in Scotland from the earliest period, in a racy, attractive style. And likewise contains an interesting Bibliography of Scottish books on Witchcraft.*

*"Sharpe was well qualified to gossip about these topics."—*SATURDAY REVIEW.

*"Mr. Sharpe has arranged all the striking and important phenomena associated with the belief in Apparitions and Witchcraft. An extensive appendix, with a list of books on Witchcraft in Scotland, and a useful index, render this edition of Mr. Sharpe's work all the more valuable."—*GLASGOW HERALD.

---

*TALES OF THE SCOTTISH PEASANTRY.* By ALEXANDER and JOHN BETHUNE. With Biography of the Authors by JOHN INGRAM, F.S.A.Scot. Post 8vo. Price 3s. 6d.

*"It is the perfect propriety of taste, no less than the thorough intimacy with the subjects he treats of, that gives Mr. Bethune's book a great charm in our eyes."—*ATHENÆUM.

*"The pictures of rural life and character appear to us remarkably true, as well as pleasing."—*CHAMBERS'S JOURNAL.

*The Tales are quite out of the ordinary routine of such literature, and are universally held in peculiarly high esteem. The following may be given as a specimen of the Contents:—" The Deformed," "The Fate of the Fairest," " The Stranger," " The Drunkard," "The Illegitimate," " The Cousins," &c., &c.*

---

*A JOURNEY TO THE WESTERN ISLANDS OF SCOTLAND IN* 1773. By SAMUEL JOHNSON, LL.D. Crown 8vo. Price 3s.

*Written by Johnson himself, and not to be confounded with Boswell's account of the same tour. Johnson said that some of his best writing is in this work.*

*THE HISTORY OF BURKE AND HARE AND OF THE RESURRECTIONIST TIMES.* A Fragment from the Criminal Annals of Scotland. By GEORGE MAC GREGOR, F.S.A.Scot. With Seven Illustrations, Demy 8vo. Price 7s. 6d.

"*Mr. MacGregor has produced a book which is eminently readable.*"—JOURNAL OF JURISPRUDENCE.

"*The book contains a great deal of curious information.*"—SCOTSMAN.

"*He who takes up this book of an evening must be prepared to sup full of horrors, yet the banquet is served with much of literary grace, and garnished with a deftness and taste which render it palatable to a degree.*"—GLASGOW HERALD.

---

*THE HISTORY OF GLASGOW:* From the Earliest Period to the Present Time. By GEORGE MAC GREGOR, F.S.A.Scot. Containing 36 Illustrations. Demy 8vo. Price 12s. 6d.

*An entirely new as well as the fullest and most complete history of this prosperous city. In addition it is the first written in chronological order. Comprising a large handsome volume in Sixty Chapters, and extensive Appendix and Index, and illustrated throughout with many interesting engravings and drawings.*

---

*THE COLLECTED WRITINGS OF DOUGAL GRAHAM,* "Skellat," Bellman of Glasgow. Edited with Notes, together with a Biographical and Bibliographical Introduction, and a Sketch of the Chap Literature of Scotland, by GEORGE MAC GREGOR, F.S.A.Scot. Impression limited to 250 copies. 2 Vols., Demy 8vo. Price 21s.

*With very trifling exceptions Graham was the only writer of purely Scottish chap-books of a secular description, almost all the others circulated being reprints of English productions. His writings are exceedingly facetious and highly illustrative of the social life of the period.*

---

*SCOTTISH PROVERBS.* By ANDREW HENDERSON. Crown 8vo. Cheaper edition. Price 2s. 6d.

*A cheap edition of a book that has long held a high place in Scottish Literature.*

*THE BOOK OF SCOTTISH ANECDOTE:* Humorous, Social, Legendary, and Historical. Edited by ALEXANDER HISLOP. Crown 8vo., pp. 768. Cheaper edition. Price 5s.

*The most comprehensive collection of Scottish Anecdotes, containing about 3,000 in number.*

---

*THE BOOK OF SCOTTISH STORY:* Historical, Traditional, Legendary, Imaginative, and Humorous. Crown 8vo., pp. 768. Cheaper edition. Price 5s.

*A most interesting and varied collection by Leading Scottish Authors.*

---

*THE BOOK OF SCOTTISH POEMS:* Ancient and Modern. Edited by J. Ross. Crown 8vo., pp. 768. Cheaper edition. Price 5s.

*Comprising a History of Scottish Poetry and Poets from the earliest times. With lives of the Poets and Selections from their Writings.*

\*\*\* These three works are uniform.

---

*A DESCRIPTION OF THE WESTERN ISLES OF SCOTLAND, CALLED HYBRIDES.* With the Genealogies of the Chief Clans of the Isles. By SIR DONALD MONRO, High Dean of the Isles, who travelled through most of them in the year 1549. Impression limited to 250 copies. Demy 8vo. Price 5s.

*This is the earliest written description of the Western Islands, and is exceedingly quaint and interesting. In this edition all the old curious spellings are strictly retained.*

---

*A DESCRIPTION OF THE WESTERN ISLANDS OF SCOTLAND CIRCA* 1695. By MARTIN MARTIN. Impression limited to 250 copies. Demy 8vo. Price 12s. 6d.

*With the exception of Dean Monro's smaller work 150 years previous, it is the earliest description of the Western Islands we have, and is the only lengthy work on the subject before the era of modern innovations. Martin very interestingly describes the people and their ways as he found them about 200 years ago.*

## THE SCOTTISH POETS, RECENT AND LIVING.
By ALEXANDER G. MURDOCH. With Portraits, Post 8vo. Price 6s.

*A most interesting resumé of Scottish Poetry in recent times. Contains a biographical sketch, choice pieces, and portraits of the recent and living Scottish Poets.*

---

## THE HUMOROUS CHAP-BOOKS OF SCOTLAND.
By JOHN FRASER. 2 Vols., Thin Crown 8vo (all published). Price 5s.

*An interesting and racy description of the chap-book literature of Scotland, and biographical sketches of the writers.*

---

## THE HISTORY OF STIRLINGSHIRE. By WILLIAM
NIMMO. 2 Vols., Demy 8vo. 3rd Edition. Price 25s.

*A new edition of this standard county history, handsomely printed, and with detailed map giving the parish boundaries and other matters of interest.*

*This county has been termed the battlefield of Scotland, and in addition to the many and important military engagements that have taken place in this district, of all which a full account is given,—this part of Scotland is of especial moment in many other notable respects,—among which particular reference may be made to the Roman Wall, the greater part of this most interesting object being situated within the boundaries of the county.*

---

## A POPULAR SKETCH OF THE HISTORY OF
GLASGOW: From the Earliest Period to the Present Time. By ANDREW WALLACE. Crown 8vo. Price 3s. 6d.

*The only attempt to write a History of Glasgow suitable for popular use.*

---

## THE HISTORY OF THE WESTERN HIGHLANDS
AND ISLES OF SCOTLAND, from A.D. 1493 to A.D. 1625. With a brief introductory sketch from A.D. 80 to A.D. 1493. By DONALD GREGORY. Demy 8vo. Price 12s. 6d.

*Incomparably the best history of the Scottish Highlands, and written purely from original investigation. Also contains particularly full and lengthened Contents and Index, respectively at beginning and end of the volume.*

*THE HISTORY OF AYRSHIRE.* By JAMES PATERSON. 5 Vols., Crown 8vo. Price 28s. net.

*The most recent and the fullest history of this exceedingly interesting county. The work is particularly rich in the department of Family History.*

---

*MARTYRLAND:* a Historical Tale of the Covenanters. By the Rev. ROBERT SIMPSON, D.D. Crown 8vo. Cheaper Edition. Price 2s. 6d.

*A tale illustrative of the history of the Covenanters in the South of Scotland.*

---

*TALES OF THE COVENANTERS.* By E. J. GUTHRIE. Crown 8vo. Cheaper Edition. Price 2s. 6d.

*A number of tales illustrative of leading incidents and characters connected with the Covenanters.*

---

*PERSONAL AND FAMILY NAMES.* A Popular Monograph on the Origin and History of the Nomenclature of the Present and Former Times. By HARRY ALFRED LONG. Demy 8vo. Price 5s.

*Interesting investigations as to the origin, history, and meaning of about 9,000 personal and family names.*

---

*THE SCOTTISH GALLOVIDIAN ENCYCLOPÆDIA* of the Original, Antiquated, and Natural Curiosities of the South of Scotland. By JOHN MACTAGGART. Demy 8vo. Price raised to 25s. Impression limited to 250 copies.

*Contains a large amount of extremely interesting and curious matter relating to the South of Scotland.*

---

*THE COMPLETE TALES OF THE ETTRICK SHEPHERD* (JAMES HOGG). 2 vols., Demy 8vo.

*An entirely new and complete edition of the tales of this popular Scottish writer.*

---

GLASGOW: THOMAS D. MORISON.
LONDON: HAMILTON, ADAMS & CO.